The Ultimate Air Fryer Cookbook UK

Affordable, Quick and Flavorful Air Fryer Recipes for Beginners | Favorites for Side Dishes, Desserts, and Snacks, Incl.

Julie C. Dutton

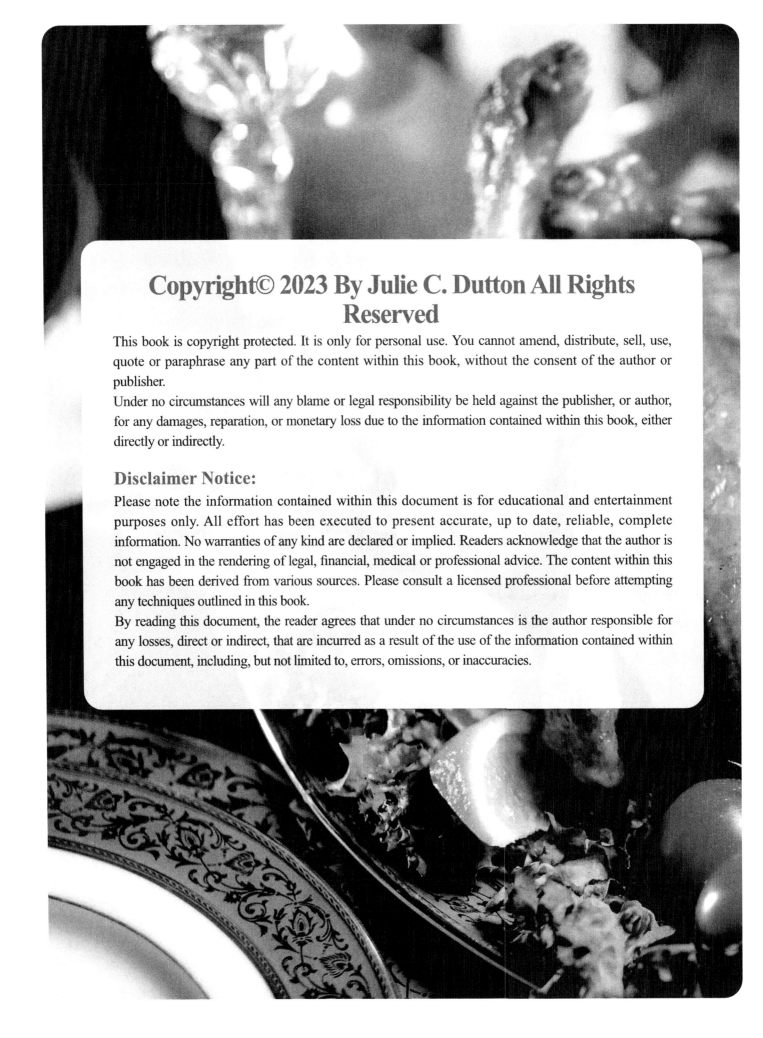

Contents

Introduction

Chapter 1 Breakfast

Chapter 2   Family Favourites

Chapter 3   Fish and Seafood

Chapter 4   Poultry

Chapter 5   Vegetarian Mains

Chapter 6   Vegetarian Vegetables and Sides

Chapter 7   Beans and Grains

Chapter 8   Pizzas, Wraps and Sandwiches

Chapter 9   Staples, Sauces, Dips and Dressings

Introduction

Air fryers are quickly becoming a go-to appliance in kitchens everywhere. They help cut fat and calories, use less oil than deep frying, cook the inside and outside of your food evenly, and cook much faster than other methods.

Air fryers cook food twice as fast and with half the calories. They're amazing, versatile kitchen machines that can be used for many things, from cooking meat to crisping-up chips and kabob sticks. What's more, it only takes about an hour to prep for a meal using an air fryer, making them perfect for busy lifestyles! If you're avid about cooking and want to tackle new recipes but don't want to sacrifice your time or hard work, then this guide will show you how.

It also takes an average of 30 minutes to make most of the recipes. There's no need to spend hours in the kitchen when you can have a delicious meal on the table in under 30 minutes. Think about how much time you spend cooking, and you'll realise that this is the best way to save time while enjoying a warm, tasty meal.

Featuring ingredients that are freely accessible in the United Kingdom was our top priority so that you won't find any foreign foods here or ingredients that would be hard to find. Every element has been chosen for its nutritional value and flavour. There are no unnecessary additives or preservatives; none of these are used in making these dishes.

You get everything here, from quick appetizers to party foods and everything in between. So whether you're trying to lose weight or looking for something new and innovative in eating out, this book has got you covered.

The Features of Air Fryer

Air fryers are equipped and designed with practical parts to streamline and ensure your cooking journey is seamless. They are also built with the latest vortex technology to bring outstanding user experiences when trying various dishes. Before using an air fryer, it is essential to understand the functionality and design of each feature of the appliance to achieve the best performance and improve its efficacy and efficiency. Here are the typical features of an air fryer:

·Temperature control button

Advanced air fryers are designed and built with temperature settings to maintain specific food recipes' temperatures. The button typically differs according to the device; for instance, most small airtight devices let up to 200 degrees Celsius/400 degrees Fahrenheit.

·Fry Yummylicious Frozen Finger Foods

Air fryers are perfect for preparing frozen foods, including French fries, mozzarella sticks, and chicken nuggets. You cannot only cook food using an air fryer but rather use it to reheat ready food making it very useful. In addition, air fryers keep the food fresh in taste and make the food crispy.

· A healthier way of coking

When purchasing an air fryer, most individuals consider the prospect of healthier cooking. With just little oil used in the cooking process, it is an excellent way of replacing deep-fried foods that are not very healthy with better alternatives.

You will spray fried foods such as fried fish and breaded chicken tenders with tiny bits of salt, and the breeding will get crispy as it cooks, thus using fewer oils. You can also cook tater tots and French fries and achieve crispy results without deep frying.

·Dishwasher safe

Another convenient feature found in some airfryers is that they are dishwasher safe, meaning all you need to do is put them in the dishwasher!

·Saves energy

Again, thanks to infrared technology, an air fryer is a great option when trying to cut down on energy use in your home or business. The lower heat and the limited use of oil reduce the amount of energy you need to cook your food. It also helps you to save on cooling costs when compared to cooking with a larger oven or stovetop.

·Non-stick coating

Many airfryers have a non-stick coating, which makes cleanup quick and easy. This also helps to prevent sticking and burning, making your cooking experience more enjoyable.

·The design makes it convenient for storage and cleanup

Who doesn't clean after cooking in the world? The truth deal is an air fryer can effectively erase the unpleasant task of wiping away in ensuring the pleasure of your meal is outstanding. As such, you will get to know that air fryers are incredibly easy to clean after being used.

Air fryers only require regular cleaning, like any pan or pot you use. You use a non-scratch sponge after adding soapy water to the basket to clean the interior and the exterior. Also, some air fryers are dishwasher safe.

Why Do I Need One?

Air fryers cook foods by convection which helps create crispy and tender food with minimal fat. Thus, air-fried food is a lot healthier than deep-fried foods. But that's not the only benefit air fryers offer.

Here are several reasons I recommend choosing an air fryer:

·Low Cost

One thing I'm sure you'll appreciate about an air fryer is that it helps you save costs. Quality cooking oil can be expensive, mainly if you're using a lot. And when using deep fryers, you'll have to add plenty of oil.

Easy to Clean

No one enjoys figuring out how an appliance works and using it forever. Air fryers make this task easier with their straightforward controls.

It gets better. Since you're the minimal amount of oil, you won't have to spend hours scrubbing the appliance. Mix soap and warm water to get your air fryer looking as good as new.

There are more benefits of an air fryer, but the ones mentioned above are some of the major benefits. You should therefore consider buying this device if you want to save on time, money and cook good food without worrying about the amount of oil being used.

What Delicious Things Can You Cook and Foods to Skipin an Air Fryer?

If there's one thing air fryers are best at, it's cooking crispy and delicious food, locked with nutrients and flavor. But if you're a newbie trying an air fryer for the first time, you're likely struggling to understand what you can cook in the air fryer.

Here's the good news: you can use air fryers to create diverse meals.One of the common concerns beginners face is: "What can I make with my Air Fryer?" The answer is "a lot". The list of things you can make with Air fryer is endless. And the best part is, you can cook most of them in less than 20 minutes.

1 Chicken wings

If you're a fan of fried chicken wings, be sure to check out our recipe for crispy air-fried wings. You'll never want to go back to the deep fryer again.

2 French fries

French fries can also be cooked in the airfryer without any oil. This makes them a healthier alternative to traditional deep-fried french fries. The airfryer will help to keep the french fries crispy on the outside while still being soft on the inside.

3 Potatoes:

Bone-in or skin-on fries and other potatoes are fantastic when you have an HOA (hot oil aversion) — throw them into your air fryer and let the electric oven do all of the work.

4 Bacon

The best way to cook bacon is by using an air fryer. An air fryer ensures the fat drips from the basket leaner, thus reducing the greasy mess. It also involves minimum supervision, unlike using an oven or stovetop.

5 Fish

Fish can be cooked in the airfryer with or without oil. If you are looking for a healthier option, you can cook your fish without any oil. The air fryer will help to keep your fish moist and tender while still getting that nice crispy exterior.

6 Zoodles

Zoodles can ideally be made from an air fryer. The food releases tons of moisture when cooking, which can help swiftly maximize drip outs in the basket, giving you perfect al dente zucchini noodles.

7 Desserts

Air frying is a great way to cook desserts! You can use your air fryer to make all sorts of delicious desserts, from cakes and cookies to brownies and pies.

Foods to Skip:

·Fresh greens

Fresh greens such as kale and spinach are food substances you should avoid putting in an air fryer. The greens will typically fly over and cook unevenly. If you want to cook fresh greens, stick to the standard ovens.

·Food with wet batter

You should avoid putting foods that contain wet natter in an air fryer, like tempura shrimp and corndogs. Wet batter revolves everywhere, and without an appropriate oil bath, the batter will not set, thus making it not crispy. The batter will make the food drip off, thus burning and sticking on the bottom of the air fryer ending up chewy.

·Most other baked goods

Sure, you can throw frozen waffles, cookies, and cakes into an air fryer and be left with a crunchy treat. But it's better to stick with baking these items in your conventional oven or get creative with swapping out ingredients or making recipes healthier. It's possible to make frozen waffles, cookies, and cakes in your air fryer if you use a thin batter. Our advice — skip the deep-fried version of these items and make healthier versions yourself!

·Breaded foods

The breading on foods like chicken nuggets or fish sticks can become too crispy in the airfryer, making them unpleasant to eat.

·Foods with sauces or gravies

Sauces and gravies can splatter and make a mess in the airfryer, so it's best to avoid them altogether.

Air Fryer Use and Maintenance

Air fryers are superb appliances that are easy to use, very convenient, and good to cook, but they may not last long if proper cleaning and maintenance are not implemented. Ensure you keep the following guidelines to achieve the value of an air fryer and make the appliance productive for some years to come.

How to clean the air fryer

1. First and foremost, unplug your air fryer from the outlet. You don't want to be working with any electrical appliances while they are still plugged in.
2. Next, you will want to remove the basket from the air fryer. Most models will have a removable basket that can easily be taken out.
3. Once the basket is removed, empty any remaining food or debris that may be inside of it.
4. After the basket is emptied, you can begin washing it with warm soapy water. Be sure to scrub any areas that look like they may need a little extra attention.
5. Once the basket is clean, set it aside and begin cleaning the interior of the air fryer itself. Again, use warm soapy water to wipe down the inside of the appliance. If there are any stubborn spots, you can use a soft sponge or brush to help remove them.
6. After you have cleaned the interior of the air fryer, dry it off with a clean towel before moving on to.

The final step is to replace the filter (if your model has one). This filter helps to keep food particles from entering into the fan area and causing damage over time. To replace it, simply remove the old filter and insert a new one.

How to maintain the air fryer

Beyond frequent cleanings of your air fryer, there are basic maintenance requirements to implement to make it function correctly and ensure it is not damaged. These requirements include the following;

1. Inspecting air fryer cords before every use. Never plug a frayed or damaged cord into an outlet since it can cause severe injuries and, in extreme cases, death. Ensure the cords are damage free and clean before using the appliance.

2. Ensure the air fryer is positioned upright, on a flat surface, before you start your cooking process.

3. Ensure the appliance is free of debris and clean before cooking. You may have left the air fryer for a long time without using it, so check inside if dust has accumulated or if there is any food residue in the basket before cooking.

4. Visually check every component of the air fryer, be it the pan, basket, and handle, to ascertain their state to contact the manufacturer and get a replacement. Putting the air fryer in enclosed areas can make it overheat.

5. Avoid placing the air fryer close to other appliances or the wall. Typically, air fryers can be placed at least 4 inches above and behind to sufficiently vent hot air and steam while cooking.

Air Fryers Safety Tips

Air fryers have become immensely popular due to their numerous benefits. With little to no oil, you can quickly fry and cook meals. Air fryers have become a go-to option for people who are on a diet or prefer healthy eating. However, these appliances come with a set of safety hazards and precautions. Here are some preventive measures you must take when using an air fryer.

·Read the manual

Go through the instructions mentioned in the manual guide before using the appliance. Air fryers can get extremely hot. Therefore, to understand its functionality, it is crucial to know everything about the appliance before plugging it in.

·Do not crowd the basket.

Even though you have a big air fryer with a large basket, as much food cannot fit the basket as you may think; food needs ample space and air circulation to ensure the food gets crispy. For instance, if you fill the basket with a whole bag of frozen fries, you won't achieve crispy food, unlike when you use half of the fries. Overcrowding the basket lengthens the cooking time in the air fryer.

·Unplug the cord after use

Keeping the plug on after using the appliance can lead to accidents. Therefore, you must immediately unplug the cord after using the appliance to avoid risking your life.

·Do not use dirty air fryer

The best way to enjoy an ideally air-fried meal is to ensure the basket is clean. Make sure you take extra care about cleaning the appliance after each use. It may sound complex and time-consuming, but keeping your appliance clean before you place meals is crucial for health. Moreover, cleaning the fryer from the inside doesn't take long; all you need is 5 minutes at most!

So, next time you prepare any meal in your air fryer, ensure you do not make these mistakes.

·Air fryers are dangerous for kids!

You should never get an air fryer for a child to use. They're not built for little hands and can pose a real safety hazard. Even if you let your child use it under your supervision, that's still a bad idea. A little one could easily burn themselves on the hot appliance, or they could set it down on the floor without realizing how hot it is when it's in use.

·Check Air Fryer Temperatures Regularly

The final safety tip — which is probably the most important one of all — is to regularly check the temperatures of your air fryer while it's in use. It's important that you don't start your appliance without knowing that the air temperature has reached at least 300 degrees Fahrenheit, and if you're using an older model — especially one that's no longer being manufactured — then make sure you do your research on how high its thermostat goes before using it.

Chapter 1   Breakfast

Breakfast Potatoes

Prep time: 5 mins
Cook time: 20 mins
Serves: 4

Ingredients:

- 500g potatoes, peeled and diced into 1 cm cubes
- 1 tsp paprika
- Salt and pepper, to taste
- 2 tbsp olive oil
- 1 tsp garlic powder

Preparation Instructions:

1. Preheat your air fryer to 200C.
2. In a large bowl, mix together the potatoes, olive oil, paprika, garlic powder, salt, and pepper.
3. Place the mixture in the air fryer basket and cook for 20-25 minutes, or until the potatoes are crispy and tender.

Omelette

Prep time: 5 mins
Cook time: 8 - 10 mins
Serves: 1

Ingredients:

- 3 eggs
- Salt and pepper, to taste
- 25 g shredded cheese
- 2 tbsp milk
- 30 g diced veggies (such as peppers, onions, and mushrooms)

Preparation Instructions:

1. Preheat your air fryer to 180C.
2. In a small bowl, beat together the eggs, milk, salt, and pepper. Add the veggies and cheese to the bowl and mix well.
3. Pour the mixture into a small cake tin and put it in the air fryer basket and cook for 8-10 minutes, or until the omelette is cooked through and the edges are crispy.

Toast Topped With Strawberry Jam

Prep time: 2 minutes
Cook time: 6 minutes
Serves 2

Ingredients:

- 4 tsp olive margarine
- 4 slices of bread (of choice)
- 4 tbsp strawberry Jam

Preparation Instructions:

1. Using a tsp or butter knife, spread margarine on each slice of bread
2. Place the bread into the air fryer at 200°C for 6-7 minutes, to make crispy toast
3. Remove the toast from air fryer and put them into a plate (2 slices per plate)
4. Dollop and spread 1 tbsp of Jam on each slice of toast before serving

Breakfast Burrito

Prep time: 5 mins
Cook time: 5- 7 mins
Serves: 2

Ingredients:

- 4 small flour tortillas
- 100 g scrambled eggs
- 60 g black beans, drained and rinsed
- 75 g diced tomato
- 60 g diced avocado
- 25 g shredded cheese
- Hot sauce, optional

Preparation Instructions:

1. Preheat your air fryer to 180C.
2. Lay out the tortillas on a flat surface.
3. Divide the eggs, black beans, tomato, avocado, and cheese evenly among the tortillas.
4. Roll the tortillas up tightly and place them seam-side down in the air fryer basket.
5. Cook for 5-7 minutes until the burritos are heated through and the edges are crispy.
6. Serve with hot sauce, if desired.

French Toast

Prep time: 5 mins
Cook time: 5- 7 mins
Serves: 2

Ingredients:

- 2 eggs
- 120 ml milk
- 1 tsp vanilla extract
- 1/2 tsp cinnamon
- 4 slices bread
- Butter, for spreading

Preparation Instructions:

1. Preheat your air fryer to 180C.
2. In a small bowl, whisk together the eggs, milk, vanilla extract, and cinnamon.
3. Dip each slice of bread into the egg mixture, making sure to coat both sides evenly.
4. Spread a thin layer of butter on one side of each slice of bread.

5. Place the bread in the air fryer basket, butter side down, and cook for 5-7 minutes, or until the French toast is golden brown.

Breakfast Quinoa

Prep time: 15 mins
Cook time: 25 mins
Serves: 2

Ingredients:

- 185 g quinoa
- 240 ml water
- 30 g diced veggies (such as peppers, onions, and mushrooms)
- 45 g diced ham
- 25 g shredded cheese.

Preparation Instructions:

1. Preheat your air fryer to 180C.
2. In a small saucepan, bring the water to a boil.
3. Add the quinoa and stir.
4. Reduce the heat to low and simmer for 15 minutes, or until the quinoa is cooked.
5. Stir in the veggies, ham, and cheese.
6. Transfer the mixture to a cake tin and put the tin into the air fryer basket and cook for 5-7 minutes, or until heated through and the cheese is melted.

Tofu Scramble

Prep time: 15 mins
Cook time: 10 - 12 mins
Serves: 2

Ingredients:

- 250g tofu, drained and crumbled
- 2 tbsp olive oil
- 35 g diced veggies (such as peppers, onions, and mushrooms)
- 1 tsp turmeric
- 1 tsp cumin
- Salt and pepper, to taste

Preparation Instructions:

1. Preheat your air fryer to 180C.
2. In a small bowl, mix together the tofu, olive oil, veggies, turmeric, cumin, salt, and pepper.
3. Transfer the mixture to the air fryer basket and cook for 10-12 minutes, or until the tofu is heated through and the edges are crispy.

Banana & Peanut butter Bagel

Prep time: 2 minutes
Cook time: 6 minutes

Serves 2

Ingredients:

- 2 cinnamon and raisin bagels
- 2 tbsp crunchy peanut butter
- 4 tsp olive margarine
- 2 large bananas

Preparation Instructions:

1. Using a kitchen knife, cut the bagels horizontally to create 2 sliced halves
2. Spread 1 tsp of margarine on the inside of each sliced bagels
3. Place the bagels in the air fryer at 200°C for 6-7 minutes (crust layers facing down)
4. Meanwhile, peel and mash the bananas and set aside as 2 portions
5. Remove the bagels from the air fryer and put them on a plate (1 bagel per plate)
6. Inside each bagel, layer one side with 1 tbsp of peanut butter and the other side with mashed banana
7. Sandwich the bagel together and serve

Breakfast Energy Balls

Prep time: 5 mins
Cook time: 5 - 7 mins
Serves: 5

Ingredients:

- 80 g rolled oats
- 1 tsp vanilla extract
- 70 g almond butter
- 35 g chocolate chips
- 130 g honey
- 25 g shredded coconut

Preparation Instructions:

1. In a medium bowl, mix together the oats, almond butter, honey, vanilla extract, chocolate chips, and coconut.
2. Roll the mixture into balls and place them in the air fryer basket.
3. Preheat your air fryer to 180C and cook the balls for 5-7 minutes, or until heated through.

Banana Bread

Prep time: 15 mins
Cook time: 30 - 35 mins
Serves: 6 - 8

Ingredients:

- 125 g plain flour
- 1/2 teaspoon salt
- 60 g unsalted butter, melted
- 1 large egg
- 1 teaspoon baking powder
- 60 g granulated sugar
- 2 medium bananas, mashed (about 200 g)
- 1 teaspoon vanilla extract

Preparation Instructions:

1. Preheat your air fryer to 180C.
2. In a large mixing bowl, whisk together the flour, baking powder, and salt.
3. In a separate bowl, whisk together the sugar, melted butter, mashed bananas, egg, and vanilla extract.
4. Pour the wet Ingredients into the dry Ingredients and stir until just combined.
5. Pour the batter into a greased loaf pan that fits inside your air fryer.
6. Cook the banana bread in the preheated air fryer for 30-35 minutes, or until a toothpick inserted into the centre comes out clean.
7. Let the banana bread cool in the pan for a few minutes before removing and slicing.

Blueberry Muffins

Prep time: 15 mins
Cook time: 12 - 15 mins
Serves: 6 - 8

Ingredients:

- 120 g plain flour
- 1/4 teaspoon salt
- 60 g unsalted butter, melted
- 1 teaspoon vanilla extract
- 1 teaspoon baking powder
- 60 g granulated sugar
- 120 ml milk
- 120 g blueberries

Preparation Instructions:

1. Preheat your air fryer to 180C.
2. In a large mixing bowl, whisk together the flour, baking powder, and salt.
3. In a separate bowl, whisk together the sugar, melted butter, milk, and vanilla extract.
4. Pour the wet Ingredients into the dry Ingredients and stir until just combined.
5. Gently fold in the blueberries.
6. Divide the muffin batter evenly among a muffin tin that fits inside your air fryer.
7. Cook the muffins in the preheated air fryer for 12-15 minutes, or until a toothpick inserted into the centre of a muffin comes out clean.
8. Let the muffins cool in the tin for a few minutes before removing and serving.

Sweet Potato Hash Browns

Prep time: 10 mins
Cook time: 8 - 10 mins
Serves: 4

Ingredients:

- 1 large sweet potato, peeled and grated
- Salt, to taste
- 1 tablespoon plain flour
- Pepper, to taste

- Cooking spray

Preparation Instructions:

1. In a large bowl, mix together the grated sweet potato, flour, salt, and pepper. Preheat your air fryer to 180C.
2. Spray the air fryer basket with cooking spray. Scoop spoonfuls of the sweet potato mixture into the basket, flattening them into patties as you go.
3. Cook the hash browns in the preheated air fryer for 8-10 minutes, or until they are crispy and golden brown on the outside.
4. Serve the hash browns hot.

Porridge Bread

Prep time: 1 hr 30 mins
Cook time: 30 - 40 mins
Serves: 8

Ingredients:

- 200 g rolled oats
- 3 g active dry yeast
- 350 ml water
- 25 g honey or maple syrup (optional, for sweetness)
- 5 g salt

Preparation Instructions:

1. In a medium-sized mixing bowl, combine the rolled oats, water, salt, and yeast. If you are using honey or maple syrup, add it now as well. Mix everything together until well combined.
2. Let the mixture sit at room temperature for at least 1 hour, or until it has doubled in size. The exact time will depend on the temperature and humidity in your kitchen, so you may need to adjust the time accordingly.
3. Preheat your air fryer to 190 °C.
4. Once the mixture has risen, use your hands to shape it into a loaf. You can either form it into a round shape or an oval shape, depending on your preference.
5. Place the loaf into the air fryer basket, making sure to leave enough space around it for the hot air to circulate.
6. Cook the bread for 30-40 minutes, or until it has formed a crust and sounds hollow when tapped on the bottom.
7. Remove the bread from the air fryer and allow it to cool for at least 15 minutes before slicing and serving.
8. The bread can be stored in a sealed container for up to 3 days at room temperature, or it can be frozen for later use.

Egg Cups

Prep time: 5 mins
Cook time: 0 mins
Serves: 4

Ingredients:

- 6 large eggs
- Salt and pepper, to taste
- 30 g shredded cheese (cheddar, mozzarella, or a combination)
- Optional fillings: diced vegetables, cooked bacon or sausage, chopped herbs or spring onions

Preparation Instructions:

1. Preheat your air fryer to 180 °C.
2. Grease the cups of a muffin tin or use a silicone one.
3. Crack one egg into each muffin cup.
4. If desired, add in any fillings (vegetables, cooked meats, herbs) to each cup.
5. Sprinkle shredded cheese over the top of each egg.
6. Season the eggs with salt and pepper to taste.
7. Carefully place the muffin tin in the air fryer basket. Cook the eggs for 7-9 minutes, or until the whites are set and the yolks are cooked to your desired level of doneness.
8. Remove the muffin tin from the air fryer and let the eggs cool for a few minutes before removing them from the tin.
9. Serve the egg cups warm.

Granola

Prep time: 5 mins
Cook time: 10 - 15 mins
Serves: 6

Ingredients:

- 1.3 kg rolled oats
- 230 g chopped nuts (almonds, walnuts, pecans, etc.)
- 115 g shredded coconut
- 60 g maple syrup or honey
- 30 g oil (coconut, avocado, or vegetable oil)
- 5 ml vanilla extract
- ½ tsp salt
- 230 g dried fruit (raisins, cranberries, blueberries, etc.) (optional)

Preparation Instructions:

1. In a large bowl, mix together the oats, nuts, and coconut.
2. In a separate bowl, mix together the maple syrup or honey, oil, vanilla extract, and salt.
3. Pour the wet Ingredients over the dry Ingredients and stir until everything is evenly coated.
4. Spread the mixture evenly in the basket of the air fryer.
5. Cook at 150°C for 10-15 minutes, stirring every 5 minutes, or until the granola is golden

brown and crispy.

6. If desired, add the dried fruit during the last minute of cooking to prevent burning.

7. Carefully remove the granola from the air fryer and let it cool completely before storing it in an airtight container.

Airfryer Baked Oats

Prep time: 5 mins
Cook time: 20 - 25 mins
Serves: 5

Ingredients:

- 200g rolled oats
- 2 ripe bananas (mashed)
- 2 teaspoons baking powder
- 1 teaspoon ground cinnamon
- 500ml milk
- 2 tablespoons honey or maple syrup
- 1 teaspoon vanilla extract
- A pinch of salt
- 2 eggs
- Optional: nuts, seeds, dried fruits, chocolate chips or any other desired toppings.

Preparation Instructions:

1. In a mixing bowl, combine the oats, baking powder, cinnamon, and a pinch of salt.
2. In another bowl, mix together the eggs, milk, mashed banana, honey, and vanilla extract.
3. Add the wet Ingredients to the dry Ingredients and stir until well combined.
4. Pour the mixture into a greased air fryer safe dish that can fit in your air fryer basket.
5. Top with any desired toppings (nuts, seeds, dried fruits, chocolate chips etc.)
6. Cook at 180°C for around 20-25 minutes or until golden brown and cooked through.

Oat Bran Muffins

Prep time: 10 minutes
Cook time: 10 to 12 minutes per batch
Makes 8 muffins

Ingredients:

- 160 ml oat bran
- 1 teaspoon baking powder
- 120 ml buttermilk
- 120 ml flour
- ½ teaspoon baking soda
- 1 egg
- 60 ml brown sugar
- ⅛ teaspoon salt
- 2 tablespoons rapeseed oil
- 120 ml chopped dates, raisins, or dried cranberries
- 24 paper muffin cups
- Cooking spray

Preparation Instructions:

1. Preheat the air fryer to 166°C.
2. In a large bowl, combine the oat bran, flour, brown sugar, baking powder, baking soda, and salt.

3. In a small bowl, beat together the buttermilk, egg, and oil.
4. Pour buttermilk mixture into bowl with dry Ingredients and stir just until moistened. Do not beat.
5. Gently stir in dried fruit.
6. Use triple baking cups to help muffins hold shape during baking. Spray them with cooking spray, place 4 sets of cups in air fryer basket at a time, and fill each one ¾ full of batter.
7. Cook for 10 to 12 minutes, until top springs back when lightly touched and toothpick inserted in center comes out clean. 8. Repeat for remaining muffins.

Breakfast Cookies

Prep time: 5 mins
Cook time: 10 - 12 mins
Serves: 6

Ingredients:

- 150g rolled oats
- 2 tablespoons honey or maple syrup
- 1 teaspoon vanilla extract
- A pinch of salt
- 50g plain flour
- 2 teaspoons baking powder
- 1 teaspoon ground cinnamon
- 1 ripe banana (mashed)
- Optional: nuts, seeds, dried fruits, chocolate chips or any other desired toppings

Preparation Instructions:

1. In a mixing bowl, combine the oats, flour, baking powder, cinnamon, and a pinch of salt.
2. In another bowl, mix together the mashed banana, honey, vanilla extract, and any desired toppings (nuts, seeds, dried fruits, chocolate chips etc.)
3. Add the wet Ingredients to the dry Ingredients and stir until well combined.
4. Use a cookie scoop or spoon to form the dough into balls, then flatten them slightly to form cookies.
5. Place the cookies in a greased and lined air fryer basket and cook at 180°C for around 10-12 minutes or until golden brown.
6. Carefully remove the cookies from the air fryer and let them cool on a wire rack before serving.

Chapter 2   Family Favourites

Fish and Chips

Prep time: 10 mins
Cook time: 45 mins
Serves: 4

Ingredients:

- 600g fish fillets, cut into strips
- Salt and pepper, to taste
- Spices of your choice (paprika, garlic powder, cayenne pepper, etc.)
- 100g flour
- 2 eggs, beaten
- 200g breadcrumbs
- 800g potatoes, cut into wedges

Preparation Instructions:

1. Cut fish fillets into strips and season with salt, pepper, and your favourite spices.
2. Dip the fish in a mixture of flour and beaten egg, then coat with breadcrumbs.
3. Cook in the air fryer at 180°C for around 10-12 minutes, or until golden brown and cooked through.
4. Peel and cut potatoes into wedges, season with salt, pepper, and your favourite spices.
5. Cook in the air fryer at 180°C for around 20-25 minutes, or until crispy and golden brown.

Meatballs

Prep time: 5 mins
Cook time: 10 - 15 mins mins
Serves: 4

Ingredients:

- 500g minced meat (beef, pork, turkey, or a mix)
- 100g breadcrumbs
- 50g grated Parmesan cheese
- 2 cloves garlic, minced
- 1 egg

Preparation Instructions:

1. Mix together minced meat, breadcrumbs, grated Parmesan cheese, minced garlic, and an egg.
2. Form into meatballs and cook in the air fryer at 180°C for around 10-15 minutes, or until cooked through.

BBQ Ribs

Prep time: 5 mins
Cook time: 30 mins mins
Serves: 4

Ingredients:

- 1 rack of pork or beef ribs
- Your favourite BBQ rub or marinade

Preparation Instructions:

1. Season a rack of pork or beef ribs with your favourite BBQ rub or marinade.
2. Cook in the air fryer at 180°C for around 25-30 minutes per side or until the meat is tender and falling off the bone.

Airfryer Fried Rice

Prep time: 20 mins
Cook time: 10 - 15 mins mins
Serves: 4

Ingredients:

- 250g cooked rice
- 100g diced vegetables
- 75g diced cooked meat
- 2 eggs
- 2 tablespoons soy sauce

Preparation Instructions:

1. Cook your favourite type of rice and let it cool down.
2. Stir fry diced vegetables, cooked meat, and eggs in a pan, then add in the rice and soy sauce.
3. Spread the mixture in a lined air fryer basket and cook for around 10-15 minutes or until the rice is crispy.

Jalapeño and Bacon Breakfast Pizza

Prep time: 5 minutes
Cook time: 10 minutes
Serves 2

Ingredients:

- 235 ml shredded Mozzarella cheese
- 30 g cream cheese, broken into small pieces
- 4 slices cooked bacon, chopped
- 60 ml chopped pickled jalapeños
- 1 large egg, whisked
- ¼ teaspoon salt

Preparation Instructions:

1. Place Mozzarella in a single layer on the bottom of an ungreased round nonstick baking dish. Scatter cream cheese pieces, bacon, and jalapeños over Mozzarella, then pour egg evenly around baking dish.
2. Sprinkle with salt and place into air fryer basket. Adjust the temperature to 166ºC and bake for 10 minutes. When cheese is brown and egg is set, pizza will be done.
3. Let cool on a large plate 5 minutes before serving.

Stuffed Peppers

Prep time: 5 mins
Cook time: 20 - 25 mins mins
Serves: 4

Ingredients:

- 4 bell peppers, halved and seeded
- 250g cooked rice
- 250g minced meat
- 125g diced tomatoes
- 50g shredded cheese

Preparation Instructions:

1. Cut bell peppers in half and remove the seeds.
2. Stuff them with a mixture of cooked rice, minced meat, diced tomatoes, and shredded cheese.
3. Cook in the air fryer at 180°C for around 20-25 minutes or until the peppers are tender and the filling is hot and bubbly.

Burgers

Prep time: 5 mins
Cook time: 10 - 12 mins mins
Serves: 4

Ingredients:

- 500g beef mince
- 1/2 teaspoon salt
- 1/4 teaspoon black pepper
- 1/4 teaspoon garlic powder
- 1/4 teaspoon onion powder
- 4 buns
- Toppings of your choice (lettuce, tomato, cheese, ketchup, mustard, etc.)

Preparation Instructions:

1. In a mixing bowl, combine the beef mince, salt, pepper, garlic powder, and onion powder. Mix well.
2. Divide the mixture into 4 equal portions and shape each into a patty.
3. Preheat your air fryer to 200 °C.
4. Place the patties in the air fryer and cook for 8-10 minutes, or until they reach an internal temperature of 71 °C.
5. During the last minute of cooking, you can add cheese on top of the patty to melt it.
6. While the burgers are cooking, toast the buns in the air fryer or in a toaster.
7. Assemble the burgers by placing a patty on the bottom half of each bun, and adding toppings as desired.
8. Serve immediately.

Lamb Kebabs

Prep time: 10 mins
Cook time: 10 - 12 mins mins

Serves: 4 - 6

Ingredients:

- 500g lamb, cut into 2.5 cm cubes
- 1 teaspoon ground cumin
- 1/2 teaspoon salt
- 2 tablespoons olive oil
- 1 red pepper, cut into 2.5 cm chunks
- Skewers (if using wooden skewers, soak them in water for 30 minutes before using)
- 2 cloves of garlic, minced
- 1 teaspoon smoked paprika
- 1/4 teaspoon black pepper
- 1 red onion, cut into 2.5 cm chunks

Preparation Instructions:

1. In a mixing bowl, combine the lamb cubes, garlic, cumin, smoked paprika, salt, pepper and olive oil. Mix well.
2. Thread the lamb cubes, onion, and bell pepper onto skewers.
3. Preheat your air fryer to 180C
4. Place the skewers in the air fryer and cook for 10-12 minutes, turning occasionally, or until the lamb is cooked through and the vegetables are slightly charred.
5. Remove the skewers from the air fryer and let them rest for a few minutes before serving.
6. You can serve this delicious lamb kebabs with some yogurt based dips, or some herbs, or with pita bread.

Mongolian-Style Beef

Prep time: 10 minutes
Cook time: 10 minutes
Serves 4

Ingredients:

- Oil, for spraying
- 450 g bavette or skirt steak, thinly sliced
- 120 ml soy sauce
- 1 tablespoon minced garlic
- 120 ml water
- Cooked white rice or ramen noodles, for serving
- 60 ml cornflour
- 180 ml packed light brown sugar
- 2 teaspoons toasted sesame oil
- ½ teaspoon ground ginger

Preparation Instructions:

1. Line the air fryer basket with parchment and spray lightly with oil.
2. Place the cornflour in a bowl and dredge the steak until evenly coated. Shake off any excess cornflour.
3. Place the steak in the prepared basket and spray lightly with oil.
4. Roast at 200°C for 5 minutes, flip, and cook for another 5 minutes.
5. In a small saucepan, combine the brown sugar, soy sauce, sesame oil, garlic, ginger, and water and bring to a boil over medium-high heat, stirring frequently. Remove from the heat.

6. Transfer the meat to the sauce and toss until evenly coated. Let sit for about 5 minutes so the steak absorbs the flavors. Serve with white rice or ramen noodles.

Pork Chops

Prep time: 5 mins
Cook time: 20 mins mins
Serves: 4

Ingredients:

- 4 pork chops
- Salt and pepper, to taste
- Spices of your choice (paprika, garlic powder, cayenne pepper, etc.)

Preparation Instructions:

1. Season pork chops with salt, pepper, and your favourite spices.
2. Cook in the air fryer at 180°C for around 8-10 minutes per side, or until cooked through.

Pizza

Prep time: 5 mins
Cook time: 10 - 12 mins mins
Serves: 3

Ingredients:

- 1 pre-made pizza crust
- 180 ml of your favourite tomato sauce
- 120 g shredded mozzarella cheese
- Toppings of your choice (sliced mushrooms, pepperoni, onions, peppers, etc.)

Preparation Instructions:

1. Preheat your air fryer to 180C.
2. Place the pizza crust in the air fryer and cook for 3 minutes.
3. Remove the crust from the air fryer and spread the tomato sauce over it, leaving a little bit of space around the edges.
4. Add the shredded cheese and your desired toppings.
5. Return the pizza to the air fryer and cook for an additional 6-8 minutes, or until the crust is crispy and the cheese is melted.
6. Remove the pizza from the air fryer and let it cool for a few minutes before slicing and serving.

Asian Style Pork

Prep time: 5 mins
Cook time: 8 - 10 mins mins
Serves: 4 - 6

Ingredients:

- 500g pork tenderloin, thinly sliced
- 2 tablespoons soy sauce
- 1 tablespoon rice vinegar
- 1 teaspoon sesame oil
- 3 cloves of garlic, minced
- 2 tablespoons hoisin sauce
- 1 tablespoon honey
- 1/4 teaspoon black pepper

Preparation Instructions:

1. In a mixing bowl, combine the pork, garlic, soy sauce, hoisin sauce, rice vinegar, honey, sesame oil, and pepper. Mix well.
2. Preheat your air fryer to 180C.
3. Place the pork in a single layer in the air fryer and cook for 8-10 minutes or until cooked through.

Beery and Crunchy Onion Rings

Prep time: 10 minutes
Cook time: 16 minutes
Serves 2 to 4

Ingredients:

- 160 ml plain flour
- ½ teaspoon bicarbonate of soda
- ½ teaspoon freshly ground black pepper
- 180 ml beer
- 1 tablespoons olive oil
- 1 large Vidalia or sweet onion, peeled and sliced into ½-inch rings
- Cooking spray
- 1 teaspoon paprika
- 1 teaspoon salt
- 1 egg, beaten
- 350 ml breadcrumbs

Preparation Instructions:

1. Preheat the air fryer to 182°C.
2. Spritz the air fryer basket with cooking spray. Combine the flour, paprika, bicarbonate of soda, salt, and ground black pepper in a bowl. Stir to mix well.
3. Combine the egg and beer in a separate bowl. Stir to mix well. Make a well in the centre of the flour mixture, then pour the egg mixture in the well. Stir to mix everything well. Pour the breadcrumbs and olive oil in a shallow plate. Stir to mix well. Dredge the onion rings gently into the flour and egg mixture, then shake the excess off and put into the plate of breadcrumbs.
4. Flip to coat both sides well. Arrange the onion rings in the preheated air fryer. Air fry in batches for 16 minutes or until golden brown and crunchy. Flip the rings and put the bottom rings to the top halfway through.
5. Serve immediately.

Korean Style Beef

Prep time: 5 mins
Cook time: 8 - 10 mins mins
Serves: 4

Ingredients:

- 500g beef sirloin, thinly sliced
- 2 tablespoons brown sugar
- 1 tablespoon sesame oil
- 1/2 teaspoon red pepper flakes
- 2 tablespoons soy sauce
- 2 cloves of garlic, minced
- 1 tablespoon rice vinegar

Preparation Instructions:

1. In a mixing bowl, combine the beef, soy sauce, brown sugar, garlic, sesame oil, rice vinegar, and red pepper flakes. Mix well.
2. Preheat your air fryer to 180C.
3. Place the beef in a single layer in the air fryer and cook for 8-10 minutes or until cooked through.

Grilled Cheese Sandwich

Prep time: 5 mins
Cook time: 5 mins mins mins
Serves: 2

Ingredients:

- 4 slices of bread
- 4 slices of cheese (cheddar, American, mozzarella, or your choice)
- 2 tbsp butter, melted

Preparation Instructions:

1. Place 2 slices of cheese between 2 slices of bread to make a sandwich.
2. Brush the butter on the outside of the sandwich.
3. Place the sandwich in the air fryer basket, making sure not to overcrowd it.
4. Cook the sandwich at 180°C for 4-5 minutes on each side or until the bread is golden brown and the cheese is melted.

Quesadillas

Prep time: 5 mins
Cook time: 5 mins mins mins
Serves: 2

Ingredients:

- 4 flour tortillas
- 100 g shredded cheese (cheddar, mozzarella, or your choice)
- 40 g diced cooked chicken or beef (optional)
- 35 g diced pepper, onions or any vegetables you like

Preparation Instructions:

1. Place a tortilla on a plate and add the cheese, chicken or beef, bell pepper, and onions on half of the tortilla.
2. Fold the tortilla in half, pressing down gently to seal.
3. Place the quesadilla in the air fryer basket, making sure not to overcrowd it.
4. Cook the quesadilla at 180°C for 4-5 minutes on each side or until the tortilla is golden brown and the cheese is melted.

Turkey Mince Pasta Bake

Prep time: 5 minutes

Cook time: 20 minutes

Serves 2-3

- 250g turkey minced meat
- 1 tbsp flaxseed oil
- 1/8 tsp sea salt
- 450g plain boiled pasta
- 60g grated cheddar cheese
- 125g diced onions
- 1 diced yellow bell pepper
- 1/8 tsp ground black pepper
- 250ml pasta sauce

Preparation Instructions:

1. Depending on your air fryer, select the 'sear/saute' function at medium heat or use a stove and pan
2. Start by pouring oil into the barrel of the air fryer for 3-4 minutes
3. Incorporate the onions and bell pepper for 3-4 minutes
4. Toss in the minced turkey to brown, and treacle with salt/pepper
5. Dollop the pasta sauce and stir thoroughly
6. Transfer the food content into a baking dish and sprinkle the cheddar on top
7. Now set the air fryer to 180°C. Place the baking dish in the air fryer and cook for 10-12 minutes
8. Retrieve the pasta bake and serve

Macaroni and Cheese Bites

Prep time: 5 mins

Cook time: 10 - 12 mins mins mins

Serves: 4

Ingredients:

- 200 g cooked macaroni pasta
- 2 eggs
- Salt, pepper and any seasoning you like
- 100 g shredded cheese
- 55 g panko bread crumbs

Preparation Instructions:

1. In a mixing bowl combine the macaroni, cheese, eggs, salt, pepper and any other seasoning you like.
2. Form the mixture into small balls.
3. Roll the balls in the panko bread crumbs.
4. Place the mac and cheese bites in the air fryer basket, making sure not to overcrowd it.
5. Cook the mac and cheese bites at 180°C for 10-12 minutes or until golden brown and crispy.

Chicken Schnitzel Dogs

Prep time: 15 minutes
Cook time: 8 to 10 minutes
Serves 4

Ingredients:

- 60 g plain flour
- 1 teaspoon dried parsley flakes
- 1 teaspoon lemon juice
- 4 chicken breast fillets, pounded thin
- 4 whole grain hotdog buns
- 1 small Granny Smith apple, thinly sliced
- Coleslaw dressing
- ½ teaspoon salt
- ½ teaspoon thyme
- 1 teaspoon water
- Oil for misting or cooking spray
- 4 slices Gouda cheese
- 60 g shredded Savoy cabbage
- 1 teaspoon marjoram
- 1 egg
- 125 g bread crumbs

Preparation Instructions:

1. In a shallow dish, mix together the flour, salt, marjoram, parsley, and thyme.
2. In another shallow dish, beat together egg, lemon juice, and water.
3. Place bread crumbs in a third shallow dish.
4. Cut each of the flattened chicken fillets in half lengthwise.
5. Dip flattened chicken strips in flour mixture, then egg wash. Let excess egg drip off and roll in bread crumbs. Spray both sides with oil or cooking spray.
6. Air fry at 200°C for 5 minutes. Spray with oil, turn over, and spray other side.
7. Cook for 3 to 5 minutes more, until well done and crispy brown.
8. To serve, place 2 schnitzel strips on bottom of each hotdog bun. Top with cheese, sliced apple, and cabbage. Drizzle with coleslaw dressing and top with other half of bun.

Lamb Koftas

Prep time: 5 - 10 mins
Cook time: 12 - 15 mins mins mins
Serves: 4

Ingredients:

- 500g lamb mince
- 2 cloves of garlic, minced
- Salt and pepper, to taste
- 1 onion, grated
- 2 tsp ground cumin
- 1 tbsp chopped fresh mint and parsley

Preparation Instructions:

1. In a mixing bowl, combine the lamb mince, onion, garlic, cumin, salt, pepper, mint, and parsley.
2. Mix well, then form the mixture into small sausage-shaped koftas.
3. Place the koftas in the air fryer basket, making sure not to overcrowd it.
4. Cook the koftas at 180°C for 12-15 minutes or until the lamb is cooked through and golden brown.

Pork and Apple Skewers

Prep time: 5 - 10 mins
Cook time: 12 - 15 mins mins mins
Serves: 4

Ingredients:

- 455 g pork loin, cut into 2.5 cm cubes
- 60 g Dijon mustard
- 1 tablespoon olive oil
- 1 large Granny Smith apple, cut into 2.5 cm cubes
- 2 tablespoons honey
- Salt and pepper, to taste

Preparation Instructions:

1. In a mixing bowl, combine the Dijon mustard, honey, olive oil, salt, and pepper.
2. Thread the pork and apple cubes onto skewers.
3. Brush the skewers with the mustard mixture.
4. Place the skewers in the air fryer basket, making sure not to overcrowd it.
5. Cook the skewers at 180°C for 12-15 minutes or until the pork is cooked through and tender.

Chapter 3   Fish and Seafood

Lemon Garlic Salmon

Prep time: 5 - 10 mins
Cook time: 8 - 10 mins mins mins
Serves: 4

Ingredients:

- 4 salmon fillets
- 1/4 cup lemon juice
- 1/4 teaspoon black pepper
- 2 tablespoons olive oil
- 1 teaspoon dried oregano
- 2 cloves of garlic, minced
- 1/4 teaspoon salt

Preparation Instructions:

1. Preheat your air fryer to 180C.
2. In a mixing bowl, combine the olive oil, garlic, lemon juice, oregano, salt, and pepper.
3. Place the salmon fillets in the mixture and coat well.
4. Place the salmon in the air fryer and cook for 8-10 minutes, or until the fish is cooked through and the internal temperature reaches 65C.

Lemony Prawns

Prep time: 10 minutes
Cook time: 7 to 8 minutes
Serves 4

Ingredients:

- 455 g prawns, peeled and deveined
- 1½ tablespoons lemon juice
- 2 cloves garlic, finely minced
- Garlic pepper, to taste
- 4 tablespoons olive oil
- 1½ tablespoons fresh parsley, roughly chopped
- 1 teaspoon crushed red pepper flakes, or more to taste
- Sea salt flakes, to taste

Preparation Instructions:

1. Preheat the air fryer to 196ºC.
2. Toss all the Ingredients in a large bowl until the prawns are coated on all sides.
3. Arrange the prawns in the air fryer basket and air fry for 7 to 8 minutes, or until the prawns are pink and cooked through.
4. Serve warm.

Fish Fillets

Prep time: 5 - 10 mins
Cook time: 8 - 10 mins mins mins

Serves: 4

Ingredients:

- 4 white fish fillets (such as cod, tilapia, or halibut)
- 2 cloves of garlic, minced
- Salt and pepper, to taste
- 2 tbsp lemon juice
- 1 tsp dried thyme
- 1 tbsp olive oil

Preparation Instructions:

1. Mix the lemon juice, garlic, thyme, salt and pepper in a small bowl.
2. Place the fish fillets in the mixture and let them marinate for 10-15 minutes.
3. Remove the fish from the marinade and pat dry.
4. Brush the fish fillets with olive oil.
5. Place the fish fillets in the air fryer basket, making sure not to overcrowd it.
6. Cook the fish fillets at 180°C for 8-10 minutes or until the fish flakes easily with a fork.

Airfried Prawns

Prep time: 5 mins
Cook time: 8 - 10 mins mins mins
Serves: 4

Ingredients:

- 455 g large prawns, peeled and deveined
- 2 tbsp olive oil
- 1 tsp paprika
- 2 cloves of garlic, minced
- Salt and pepper, to taste
- 1 tsp dried oregano

Preparation Instructions:

1. In a mixing bowl, combine the shrimp, garlic, olive oil, salt, pepper, paprika, and oregano.
2. Toss to coat the prawns evenly.
3. Place the prawns in the air fryer basket, making sure not to overcrowd it.
4. Cook the prawns at 180°C for 8-10 minutes or until pink and cooked through.

Crab Cakes

Prep time: 10 mins
Cook time: 8 - 10 mins mins mins
Serves: 4 - 6

Ingredients:

- 455 g crabmeat
- 40 g diced red pepper
- 1 tsp paprika
- Salt and pepper, to taste
- 120 g mayonnaise
- 2 cloves of garlic, minced
- 30 g Panko breadcrumbs
- 50 g diced onion
- 2 tbsp Dijon mustard
- 1 egg

Preparation Instructions:

1. n a mixing bowl, combine the crabmeat, mayonnaise, onion, red pepper, garlic, Dijon mustard, paprika, Panko, egg, salt and pepper.
2. Mix well, then form the mixture into cakes, about 8 cm in diameter.
3. Place the crab cakes in the air fryer basket, making sure not to overcrowd it.
4. Cook the crab cakes at 180°C for 8-10 minutes or until golden brown and crispy.

Airfried Scampi

Prep time: 5 mins
Cook time: 8 - 10 mins mins mins
Serves: 4 - 6

Ingredients:

- 455 g scampi (or large prawns), peeled and deveined
- 2 tbsp olive oil
- 1 tsp garlic powder
- 1 tsp paprika
- 1/2 tsp salt
- 1/4 tsp black pepper

Preparation Instructions:

1. In a bowl, combine the scampi, olive oil, garlic powder, paprika, salt, and pepper. Toss to coat the scampi evenly.
2. Place the scampi in the air fryer basket in a single layer.
3. Set the air fryer to 200°C and cook the scampi for 8-10 minutes, or until they are pink and cooked through.
4. Serve the scampi hot with your favourite dipping sauce.

Scallops

Prep time: 5 mins
Cook time: 8 - 10 mins mins mins
Serves: 4

Ingredients:

- 455 g sea scallops
- 2 tbsp olive oil
- 1 tsp garlic powder
- 1 tsp dried parsley
- 1/2 tsp salt
- 1/4 tsp black pepper

Preparation Instructions:

1. In a small bowl, combine the olive oil, garlic powder, parsley, salt, and pepper.
2. Place the scallops in a shallow dish and brush the olive oil mixture onto both sides of the scallops.
3. Placc the scallops in the air fryer basket in a single layer.
4. Set the air fryer to 180°C and cook the scallops for 8-10 minutes, or until they are cooked through and slightly browned.
5. Serve the scallops hot with your favourite side dish or dipping sauce.

Mussels

Prep time: 15 mins
Cook time: 3 -5 mins mins mins
Serves: 4

Ingredients:

- 900 g mussels, scrubbed and debearded
- 2 cloves garlic, minced
- 60 ml chicken stock
- 2 tbsp chopped fresh parsley
- 1/4 tsp black pepper
- 2 tbsp butter
- 60 ml white wine
- 60 g cream
- 1/4 tsp salt

Preparation Instructions:

1. In a large frying pan, melt the butter over medium heat. Add the garlic and cook for 1-2 minutes, or until fragrant.
2. Add the mussels, white wine, chicken stock, cream, parsley, salt, and pepper. Stir to combine.
3. Bring the mixture to a boil, then reduce the heat to low and simmer for 5-7 minutes, or until the mussels are cooked through and open. Discard any mussels that do not open.
4. Using a slotted spoon, transfer the mussels to the air fryer basket.
5. Set the air fryer to 180°C and cook the mussels for 3-5 minutes, or until they are hot and the sauce is bubbly.
6. Serve the mussels hot with the sauce and bread to mop up the sauce.

Calamari

Prep time: 10 mins
Cook time: 8 -10 mins mins mins
Serves: 4

Ingredients:

- 455 g cleaned squid, cut into rings
- 1 tsp paprika
- 1/4 tsp black pepper
- 1 tsp garlic powder
- 1 large egg
- 60 g flour
- 1/2 tsp salt
- 50 g breadcrumbs

Preparation Instructions:

1. In a shallow dish, combine the flour, paprika, garlic powder, salt, and pepper.
2. In another shallow dish, beat the egg.
3. Place the breadcrumbs in a third shallow dish.
4. Dredge each squid ring in the flour mixture, shaking off any excess. Dip the rings into the beaten egg, then coat them with the breadcrumbs, pressing the breadcrumbs onto the rings to adhere.
5. Place the breaded squid rings in the air fryer basket.

6. Set the air fryer to 180°C and cook the squid for 8-10 minutes, or until the squid is cooked through and the breadcrumbs are golden brown.
7. Serve the calamari hot with your favourite dipping sauce.

Teriyaki Salmon

Prep time: 5 mins
Cook time: 8 -10 mins mins
Serves: 4

Ingredients:

- 4 (100 g) salmon fillets
- 1 tbsp rice vinegar
- 1 clove garlic, minced
- 60 g teriyaki sauce
- 1 tsp sesame oil
- 2 tbsp honey
- 1 tsp grated ginger

Preparation Instructions:

1. In a small bowl, combine the teriyaki sauce, honey, rice vinegar, sesame oil, ginger, and garlic.
2. Place the salmon fillets in a shallow dish and brush the teriyaki mixture onto both sides of the fillets.
3. Place the salmon in the air fryer basket in a single layer.
4. Set the air fryer to 180°C and cook the salmon for 8-10 minutes, or until the salmon is cooked through and the skin is crispy.
5. Serve the salmon hot with your favourite side dish.

Maple Mustard Salmon

Prep time: 5 mins
Cook time: 8 -10 mins mins
Serves: 4

Ingredients:

- 4 (100 g) salmon fillets
- 1 tsp dried thyme
- 2 tbsp dijon mustard
- 1/2 tsp salt
- 2 tbsp maple syrup
- 1/4 tsp black pepper

Preparation Instructions:

1. In a small bowl, combine the dijon mustard, maple syrup, thyme, salt, and pepper.
2. Place the salmon fillets in a shallow dish and brush the maple-mustard mixture onto both sides of the fillets.
3. Place the salmon in the air fryer basket in a single layer.
4. Set the air fryer to 180°C and cook the salmon for 8-10 minutes, or until the salmon is cooked through and the skin is crispy.
5. Serve the salmon hot with your favourite side dish.

Lemon Pepper Cod

Prep time: 5 mins
Cook time: 8 -10 mins mins
Serves: 4

Ingredients:

- 4 (100 g) cod fillets
- 1 tsp lemon pepper seasoning
- 2 tbsp olive oil
- 1/2 tsp salt
- 2 tbsp lemon juice
- 1/4 tsp black pepper

Preparation Instructions:

1. In a small bowl, combine the olive oil, lemon juice, lemon pepper seasoning, salt, and pepper.
2. Place the cod fillets in a shallow dish and brush the lemon pepper mixture onto both sides of the fillets.
3. Place the cod in the air fryer basket in a single layer.
4. Set the air fryer to 180°C and cook the cod for 8-10 minutes, or until the cod is cooked through and flaky.

Snapper Scampi

Prep time: 5 minutes
Cook time: 8 to 10 minutes
Serves 4

Ingredients:

- 4 (170 g) skinless snapper or arctic char fillets
- 3 tablespoons lemon juice, divided
- Pinch salt
- 2 tablespoons butter
- 1 tablespoon olive oil
- ½ teaspoon dried basil
- Freshly ground black pepper, to taste
- 2 cloves garlic, minced

Preparation Instructions:

1. Rub the fish fillets with olive oil and 1 tablespoon of the lemon juice. Sprinkle with the basil, salt, and pepper, and place in the air fryer basket.
2. Air fry the fish at 192°C for 7 to 8 minutes or until the fish just flakes when tested with a fork. Remove the fish from the basket and put on a serving plate. Cover to keep warm.
3. In a baking pan, combine the butter, remaining 2 tablespoons lemon juice, and garlic. Bake in the air fryer for 1 to 2 minutes or until the garlic is sizzling. Pour this mixture over the fish and serve

Cajun Cod

Prep time: 5 mins
Cook time: 8 -10 mins mins
Serves: 4

Ingredients:

- 4 (100 g) cod fillets
- 1 tsp dried oregano
- 2 tbsp olive oil
- 1 tsp dried thyme
- 2 tbsp Cajun seasoning
- 1/4 tsp black pepper

Preparation Instructions:

1. In a small bowl, combine the olive oil, Cajun seasoning, oregano, thyme, and pepper.
2. Place the cod fillets in a shallow dish and brush the Cajun mixture onto both sides of the fillets.
3. Place the cod in the air fryer basket in a single layer.
4. Set the air fryer to 180°C and cook the cod for 8-10 minutes, or until the cod is cooked through and flaky.

Fish Pie

Prep time: 30 mins

Cook time: 15 -20 mins mins

Serves: 4 - 6

Ingredients:

- 2 large potatoes, peeled and diced
- 100 g frozen peas
- 455 g white fish fillets, cut into bite-sized pieces
- 2 cloves of garlic, minced
- 2 tablespoons flour
- Salt and pepper, to taste
- 1 onion, diced
- 100 g frozen corn
- 240 g cream
- 2 tablespoons butter
- 1 teaspoon dried thyme
- 100 g grated cheddar cheese

Preparation Instructions:

1. Preheat your air fryer to 180C..
2. In a pot of boiling water, cook the potatoes until they are tender. Drain and set aside.
3. In a pan, sauté the onion, garlic, and thyme in butter until the onion is translucent.
4. Stir in the flour and cook for 1 minute.
5. Gradually add the cream, stirring constantly, until the mixture thickens.
6. Stir in the fish, peas, corn, and cooked potatoes.
7. Season with salt and pepper, to taste.
8. Transfer the mixture to a greased oven-safe dish that will fit in your air fryer.
9. Top with grated cheese.
10. Place the dish in the air fryer and cook for 15-20 minutes, or until the cheese is melted and bubbly.

Friday Night Fish-Fry

Prep time: 10 minutes

Cook time: 10 minutes

Serves 4

Ingredients:

- 1 large egg
- 1 teaspoon smoked paprika
- ¼ teaspoon ground black pepper
- 45 g powdered Parmesan cheese
- ¼ teaspoon celery salt
- 4 cod fillets, 110 g each
- Chopped fresh oregano or parsley, for garnish (optional)
- Lemon slices, for serving (optional)

Preparation Instructions:

1. Spray the air fryer basket with avocado oil. Preheat the air fryer to 204ºC.
2. Crack the egg in a shallow bowl and beat it lightly with a fork. Combine the Parmesan cheese, paprika, celery salt, and pepper in a separate shallow bowl.
3. One at a time, dip the fillets into the egg, then dredge them in the Parmesan mixture. Using your hands, press the Parmesan onto the fillets to form a nice crust. As you finish, place the fish in the air fryer basket.
4. Air fry the fish in the air fryer for 10 minutes, or until it is cooked through and flakes easily with a fork. Garnish with fresh oregano or parsley and serve with lemon slices, if desired.
5. Store leftovers in an airtight container in the refrigerator for up to 3 days. Reheat in a preheated 204ºC air fryer for 5 minutes, or until warmed through.

Fish Fingers

Prep time: 5 mins
Cook time: 8 -10 mins mins
Serves: 4 - 6

Ingredients:

- 500g white fish fillets, cut into finger-sized pieces
- 1 teaspoon paprika
- 1/2 teaspoon salt
- 2 eggs, beaten
- 30g grated Parmesan cheese
- 125g plain flour
- 1 teaspoon garlic powder
- 1/4 teaspoon black pepper
- 125g breadcrumbs

Preparation Instructions:

1. Preheat your air fryer to 180°C.
2. In a shallow dish, combine the flour, paprika, garlic powder, salt, and pepper.
3. In a separate shallow dish, beat the eggs.
4. In another shallow dish, mix together the breadcrumbs and grated Parmesan cheese.
5. Dip each fish finger in the flour mixture, then the beaten eggs, and finally the breadcrumb mixture, pressing the breadcrumbs onto the fish to adhere.
6. Place the fish fingers in the air fryer basket, making sure they are not overcrowded.
7. Cook the fish fingers for 8-10 minutes or until golden brown and cooked through.

Airfryer Mackerel

Prep time: 5 mins
Cook time: 8 -10 mins mins
Serves: 4

Ingredients:

- 4 mackerel fillets
- 2 cloves of garlic, minced
- 1 teaspoon paprika
- 2 tablespoons olive oil
- 2 teaspoons dried oregano
- Salt and pepper, to taste

Preparation Instructions:

1. Preheat your air fryer to 180°C.
2. In a small bowl, mix together the olive oil, garlic, oregano, paprika, salt and pepper.
3. Place the mackerel in a shallow dish and brush the seasoning mixture on both sides of the fish.
4. Place the fish in the air fryer basket, making sure they are not overcrowded.
5. Cook the fish for 8-10 minutes or until cooked through and the skin is crispy.

Kung Pao Chicken

Prep time: 5 mins
Cook time: 8 -10 mins mins
Serves: 4

Ingredients:

- 500g boneless, skinless chicken thighs, diced
- 2 tablespoons soy sauce
- 2 teaspoons sugar
- 2 cloves of garlic, minced
- 1/4 teaspoon red pepper flakes
- 1 red pepper, diced
- 2 tablespoons cornflour
- 1 tablespoon rice vinegar
- 1 teaspoon sesame oil
- 1 teaspoon grated ginger
- 2 tablespoons vegetable oil
- 30 g unsalted peanuts

Preparation Instructions:

1. In a mixing bowl, combine the chicken, cornflour, soy sauce, rice vinegar, sugar, sesame oil, garlic, ginger, and red pepper flakes. Mix well.
2. Preheat your air fryer to 180C.
3. Place the chicken in a single layer in the air fryer and cook for 8-10 minutes or until cooked through.

Italian Flavour Chicken Breasts

Prep time: 10 minutes
Cook time: 60 minutes
Serves 8

Ingredients:

- 1.4 kg chicken breasts, bone-in
- 1 teaspoon minced fresh rosemary
- 1 teaspoon cayenne pepper
- ½ teaspoon freshly ground black pepper
- Cooking spray
- 1 teaspoon minced fresh basil
- 2 tablespoons minced fresh parsley
- ½ teaspoon salt
- 4 medium Roma tomatoes, halved

Preparation Instructions:

1. Preheat the air fryer to 190°C. Spritz the air fryer basket with cooking spray.
2. Combine all the Ingredients, except for the chicken breasts and tomatoes, in a large bowl. Stir to mix well.
3. Dunk the chicken breasts in the mixture and press to coat well.
4. Transfer the chicken breasts in the preheated air fryer. You may need to work in batches to avoid overcrowding.

5. Air fry for 25 minutes or until the internal temperature of the thickest part of the breasts reaches at least 76ºC. Flip the breasts halfway through the cooking time.

6. Remove the cooked chicken breasts from the basket and adjust the temperature to 180ºC.

7. Place the tomatoes in the air fryer and spritz with cooking spray. Sprinkle with a touch of salt and cook for 10 minutes or until tender. Shake the basket halfway through the cooking time.

8. Serve the tomatoes with chicken breasts on a large serving plate.

Lemon Herbed Chicken

Prep time: 30 + mins
Cook time: 15 -20 mins mins
Serves: 4

Ingredients:

- 4 boneless, skinless chicken breasts (about 600g)
- 2 cloves of garlic, minced
- 1 tbsp fresh thyme leaves
- 1/2 tsp black pepper
- 2 tbsp olive oil
- 1 tbsp fresh lemon zest
- 1 tsp salt

Preparation Instructions:

1. In a small bowl, mix together the olive oil, garlic, lemon zest, thyme, salt, and pepper.
2. Place the chicken breasts in a large resealable plastic bag or a shallow dish.
3. Pour the marinade over the chicken, making sure that each breast is coated evenly. Marinate for at least 30 minutes or up to 2 hours in the refrigerator.
4. Preheat the air fryer to 180°C.
5. Place the chicken breasts in the air fryer basket, making sure they are not touching.
6. Cook the chicken for 15-20 minutes, or until the internal temperature reaches 74°C.

Chicken and Ham Meatballs with Dijon Sauce

Prep time: 10 minutes
Cook time: 15 minutes
Serves 4

Ingredients:

Meatballs:

- 230 g ham, diced
- 110 g grated Swiss cheese
- 3 cloves garlic, minced
- 1½ teaspoons sea salt
- Cooking spray
- 230 g chicken mince
- 1 large egg, beaten
- 15 g chopped onions
- 1 teaspoon ground black pepper

Dijon Sauce:

- 3 tablespoons Dijon mustard
- 2 tablespoons lemon juice

- 60 ml chicken broth, warmed
- ¼ teaspoon ground black pepper
- ¾ teaspoon sea salt
- Chopped fresh thyme leaves, for garnish

Preparation Instructions:

1. Preheat the air fryer to 200°C. Spritz the air fryer basket with cooking spray.
2. Combine the Ingredients for the meatballs in a large bowl. Stir to mix well, then shape the mixture in twelve 1½-inch meatballs.
3. Arrange the meatballs in a single layer in the air fryer basket. Air fry for 15 minutes or until lightly browned. Flip the balls halfway through. You may need to work in batches to avoid overcrowding.
4. Meanwhile, combine the Ingredients, except for the thyme leaves, for the sauce in a small bowl. Stir to mix well.
5. Transfer the cooked meatballs on a large plate, then baste the sauce over. Garnish with thyme leaves and serve.

Crispy Chicken Tenders

Prep time: 10 mins
Cook time: 12 -15 mins mins
Serves: 4 - 6

Ingredients:

- 800g chicken tenders
- 1 tsp garlic powder
- 2 eggs
- 125 g flour
- 1 tsp salt
- 110 g panko breadcrumbs
- 2 tsp paprika
- 1/2 tsp black pepper

Preparation Instructions:

1. In a shallow dish, mix together the flour, paprika, garlic powder, salt, and pepper.
2. In a separate shallow dish, beat the eggs.
3. Place the panko breadcrumbs in a third shallow dish.
4. Dip each chicken tender in the flour mixture, then the eggs, then the breadcrumbs, making sure that each tender is coated evenly.
5. Preheat the air fryer to 180°C.
6. Place the chicken tenders in the air fryer basket, making sure they are not touching.
7. Cook the chicken tenders for 12-15 minutes, or until the internal temperature reaches 74°C and the breading is golden brown and crispy.

BBQ Turkey Breast

Prep time: 10 mins
Cook time: 50 - 60 mins mins
Serves: 6 - 8

Ingredients:

- 1 turkey breast (about 1 kg)
- 1 tsp smoked paprika
- 60 g BBQ sauce
- 1 tsp garlic powder
- 1 tbsp brown sugar
- Salt and pepper, to taste

Preparation Instructions:

1. Mix together the BBQ sauce, brown sugar, paprika, garlic powder, salt, and pepper in a small bowl.
2. Place the turkey breast in the air fryer and brush the mixture over the turkey.
3. Cook at 180C for 20-25 minutes per 500g, or until the internal temperature reaches 74C.

Maple Glazed Turkey

Prep time: 10 mins

Cook time: 50 - 60 mins mins

Serves: 6 - 8

Ingredients:

- 1 turkey breast (about 1 kg)
- 1 tsp dried sage
- 75 g maple syrup
- Salt and pepper, to taste
- 2 tbsp Dijon mustard

Preparation Instructions:

1. Mix together the maple syrup, mustard, sage, salt, and pepper in a small bowl.
2. Place the turkey breast in the air fryer and brush the mixture over the turkey.
3. Cook at 180 °C for 20-25 minutes per 500g, or until the internal temperature reaches 74 °C.

Chicken Breasts with Asparagus and Beans

Prep time: 20 minutes

Cook time: 25 minutes

Serves 2

Ingredients:

- 125 g canned cannellini beans, rinsed
- 1 garlic clove, minced
- Salt and ground black pepper, to taste
- 230 g asparagus, trimmed and cut into 1-inch lengths
- 2 (230 g) boneless, skinless chicken breasts, trimmed
- ¼ teaspoon paprika
- 60 g baby rocket, rinsed and drained
- 1½ tablespoons red wine vinegar
- 2 tablespoons extra-virgin olive oil, divided
- ½ red onion, sliced thinly
- ½ teaspoon ground coriander

Preparation Instructions:

1. Preheat the air fryer to 204ºC.
2. Warm the beans in microwave for 1 minutes and combine with red wine vinegar, garlic,

1 tablespoon of olive oil, ¼ teaspoon of salt, and ¼ teaspoon of ground black pepper in a bowl. Stir to mix well.

3. Combine the onion with ⅛ teaspoon of salt, ⅛ teaspoon of ground black pepper, and 2 teaspoons of olive oil in a separate bowl. Toss to coat well.

4. Place the onion in the air fryer and air fry for 2 minutes, then add the asparagus and air fry for 8 more minutes or until the asparagus is tender. Shake the basket halfway through. Transfer the onion and asparagus to the bowl with beans. Set aside.

5. Toss the chicken breasts with remaining Ingredients, except for the baby arugula, in a large bowl.

6. Put the chicken breasts in the air fryer and air fry for 14 minutes or until the internal temperature of the chicken reaches at least 76°C. Flip the breasts halfway through.

7. Remove the chicken from the air fryer and serve on an aluminum foil with asparagus, beans, onion, and rocket. Sprinkle with salt and ground black pepper. Toss to serve.

Chicken Kiev

Prep time: 10 mins
Cook time: 20 - 25 mins
Serves: 4

Ingredients:

- 4 chicken breasts
- 4 tablespoons of butter, at room temperature
- Salt and pepper, to taste
- 2 eggs, beaten
- Oil, for brushing
- 4 cloves of garlic, minced
- 1 teaspoon of dried parsley
- 125 g flour
- 100 g breadcrumbs

Preparation Instructions:

1. Preheat the air fryer to 180 °C.
2. In a small bowl, mix together the minced garlic, butter, dried parsley, salt and pepper.
3. Place the chicken breasts between two sheets of plastic wrap and pound them with a meat mallet until they are an even thickness.
4. Place a spoonful of the butter mixture on one end of each chicken breast and roll them up, tucking in the ends to seal the butter inside.
5. Place the flour, beaten eggs, and breadcrumbs in separate shallow bowls.
6. Dip each chicken breast in the flour, then the eggs, and finally the breadcrumbs, making sure they are well coated.
7. Brush the chicken with a little oil and place them in the air fryer.
8. Cook for 20-25 minutes, or until the chicken is cooked through and the breadcrumbs are golden brown.
9. Remove from the air fryer and let them rest for a few minutes before serving.

Buttermilk Chicken

Prep time: 10 mins
Cook time: 15 - 20 mins
Serves: 4

Ingredients:

- 4 boneless chicken thighs
- 125 g flour
- 1 teaspoon of paprika
- 1 teaspoon of garlic powder
- 1 teaspoon of onion powder
- Salt and pepper, to taste
- 240 ml buttermilk
- Oil, for brushing

Preparation Instructions:

1. Preheat the air fryer to 180 °C.
2. In a shallow dish, mix together the flour, paprika, garlic powder, onion powder, salt and pepper.
3. Place the buttermilk in a separate shallow dish.
4. Dip each chicken thigh in the buttermilk, then coat in the flour mixture, pressing the flour mixture onto the chicken to make sure it sticks.
5. Brush the chicken with a little oil and place them in the air fryer.
6. Cook for 15-20 minutes, or until the chicken is cooked through and the coating is golden brown.
7. Remove from the air fryer and let them rest for a few minutes before serving.

Parmesan Crusted Chicken

Prep time: 10 mins
Cook time: 15 - 20 mins
Serves: 4

Ingredients:

- 4 boneless chicken breasts
- 50 g grated Parmesan cheese
- 65 g flour
- 2 eggs, beaten
- 100 g breadcrumbs
- Salt and pepper, to taste
- Oil, for brushing

Preparation Instructions:

1. Preheat the air fryer to 180 °C.
2. Place the grated Parmesan cheese, flour, beaten eggs, breadcrumbs, salt and pepper in separate shallow bowls.
3. Dip each chicken breast in the flour, then the eggs, and finally the breadcrumbs, pressing the breadcrumbs onto the chicken to make sure they stick.
4. Brush the chicken with a little oil and place them in the air frycr.
5. Cook for 15-20 minutes, or until the chicken is cooked through and the coating is golden brown.
6. Remove from the air fryer and let them rest for a few minutes before serving.

Duck Breast

Prep time: 5 mins
Cook time: 8-10 mins
Serves: 2

Ingredients:

- 2 duck breasts
- Salt and pepper, to taste
- Oil, for brushing

Preparation Instructions:

1. Preheat the air fryer to 180 °C.
2. Score the duck skin in a crosshatch pattern, being careful not to cut into the meat.
3. Season the duck breasts with salt and pepper on both sides.
4. Place the duck breasts, skin side down, in the air fryer.
5. Cook for 8-10 minutes, or until the skin is crispy and the meat is cooked to your desired level of doneness.
6. Remove from the air fryer and let them rest for a few minutes before slicing and serving.

Duck Leg

Prep time: 10 mins
Cook time: 30-40 mins
Serves: 4

Ingredients:

- 4 duck legs
- 1 teaspoon of dried rosemary
- 2 cloves of garlic, minced
- Salt and pepper, to taste
- 1 teaspoon of dried thyme
- Oil, for brushing

Preparation Instructions:

1. Preheat the air fryer to 180 °C.
2. In a small bowl, mix together the minced garlic, dried thyme, dried rosemary, salt and pepper.
3. Rub the mixture all over the duck legs, making sure to coat them evenly.
4. Brush the duck legs with a little oil and place them in the air fryer.
5. Cook for 30-40 minutes, or until the skin is crispy and the meat is cooked through.
6. Remove from the air fryer and let them rest for a few minutes before serving.

Kentucky Air Fried Chicken Wings

Prep time: 10 minutes
Cook time: 30 minutes
Serves 4

Ingredients

- 1400g of chicken wings (15-16 wings)
- 2 large eggs
- 240g all-purpose flour
- 2 tsp garlic powder
- 2 tsp onion powder
- 1 tsp ground black pepper
- 350ml buttermilk
- 3 tsp paprika
- 2 tsp salt
- 1cal olive oil spray

Preparation Instructions:

1. Preheat the air fryer at 180°C for 3-4 minutes
2. Amalgamate the buttermilk and eggs in a stand mixer
3. Using a small bowl, combine all of the dry Ingredients to make the coating flour
4. Employing some kitchen tongs, submerge each chicken wings in the flour, followed by the buttermilk, then back into the flour
5. Place the chicken in the air fryer and cover it with the fry spray
6. Preferably select the 'air crisp' function or cook the chicken at 180°C for 20 minutes
7. Shake the chicken wings and cook for another 5 minutes
8. Retrieve the chicken wings and place them into a dish, then serve

Orange Glazed Duck

Prep time: 5-10 mins
Cook time: 15 mins
Serves: 2

Ingredients:

- 2 duck breasts
- 70 g orange marmalade
- 2 tablespoons of soy sauce
- 1 tablespoon of honey
- 1/2 teaspoon of black pepper
- Oil, for brushing

Preparation Instructions:

1. Preheat the air fryer to 180 °C.
2. In a small bowl, mix together the orange marmalade, soy sauce, honey and black pepper.
3. Score the duck skin in a crosshatch pattern, being careful not to cut into the meat.
4. Brush the duck breasts with a little oil and place them in the air fryer, skin side down.
5. Cook for 8-10 minutes or until the skin is crispy.
6. Brush the glaze over the duck breasts and cook for an additional 2-3 minutes or until the glaze is caramelized.
7. Remove from the air fryer and let them rest for a few minutes before slicing and serving.

Five Spiced Duck

Prep time: 5-10 mins
Cook time: 8-10 mins
Serves: 2

Ingredients:

- 2 duck breasts
- 1 tablespoon of honey
- 1 teaspoon of five-spice powder
- 1 clove of garlic, minced
- 1 tablespoon of soy sauce
- Oil, for brushing

Preparation Instructions:

1. Preheat the air fryer to 180 °C.
2. In a small bowl, mix together the five-spice powder, soy sauce, honey, minced garlic and some oil.
3. Score the duck skin in a crosshatch pattern, being careful not to cut into the meat.
4. Rub the marinade all over the duck breasts, making sure to coat them evenly.
5. Place the duck breasts, skin side down, in the air fryer.
6. Cook for 8-10 minutes or until the skin is crispy and the meat is cooked to your desired level of doneness.
7. Remove from the air fryer and let them rest for a few minutes before slicing and serving.

Spicy Turkey

Prep time: 5-10 mins
Cook time: 20 - 25 mins
Serves: 4

Ingredients:

- 1 turkey breast, butterflied
- 1 teaspoon of cumin
- 2 tablespoons of olive oil
- 1 teaspoon of garlic powder
- 1 teaspoon of chili powder
- Salt and pepper, to taste

Preparation Instructions:

1. Preheat the air fryer to 180 °C.
2. In a small bowl, mix together the olive oil, chili powder, cumin, garlic powder, salt, and pepper.
3. Rub the mixture all over the turkey breast, making sure to coat it evenly.
4. Place the turkey breast in the air fryer.
5. Cook for 20-25 minutes, or until the turkey is cooked through.
6. Remove from the air fryer and let it rest for a few minutes before slicing and serving.

Citrus and Herb Turkey Breast

Prep time: 5-10 mins
Cook time: 20 - 25 mins
Serves: 4

Ingredients:

- 1 turkey breast, butterflied
- 1 teaspoon of dried oregano
- 2 tablespoons of olive oil
- 1 teaspoon of dried sage
- 1 teaspoon of dried thyme
- zest of 1 orange

• zest of 1 lemon   • Salt and pepper, to taste

Preparation Instructions:

1. Preheat the air fryer to 180 °C.
2. In a small bowl, mix together the olive oil, dried thyme, dried oregano, dried sage, orange zest, lemon zest, salt, and pepper.
3. Rub the mixture all over the turkey breast, making sure to coat it evenly.
4. Place the turkey breast in the air fryer.
5. Cook for 20-25 minutes, or until the turkey is cooked through.
6. Remove from the air fryer and let it rest for a few minutes before slicing and serving.

Tandoori Chicken

Prep time: 30 + mins
Cook time: 15 - 20 mins
Serves: 4

Ingredients:

• 4 boneless chicken breasts   • 480 g plain yogurt   • 2 tablespoons of tandoori masala
• 2 cloves of garlic, minced   • Salt and pepper, to taste   • Oil, for brushing

Preparation Instructions:

1. Preheat the air fryer to 180 °C.
2. In a small bowl, mix together the yogurt, tandoori masala, minced garlic, salt, and pepper.
3. Place the chicken breasts in a large resealable bag and pour the tandoori yogurt mixture over them. Seal the bag and toss to coat the chicken. Marinate for at least 30 minutes or overnight in the refrigerator.
4. Brush the chicken with a little oil and place them in the air fryer.
5. Cook for 15-20 minutes, or until the chicken is cooked through and the coating is golden brown

Chapter 5　Vegetarian Mains

Tofu

Prep time: 30 + mins
Cook time: 15 - 20 mins
Serves: 4

Ingredients:

- 400g extra-firm tofu, drained and pressed
- 2 tablespoons of hoisin sauce
- 1 teaspoon of grated ginger
- 1 tablespoon of cornflour
- 2 tablespoons of soy sauce
- 2 cloves of garlic, minced
- 1 teaspoon of sesame oil

Preparation Instructions:

1. Preheat the air fryer to 180 °C.
2. In a small bowl, mix together the soy sauce, hoisin sauce, minced garlic, grated ginger, sesame oil, and cornflour.
3. Cut the tofu into cubes and place them in a large resealable bag. Pour the marinade over the tofu and toss to coat. Let it marinate for at least 30 minutes or overnight in the refrigerator.
4. Place the tofu cubes in the air fryer and cook for 15-20 minutes, or until crispy and golden brown, turning halfway through.
5. Remove from the air fryer and serve with your favourite dipping sauce.

Cauliflower Steaks

Prep time: 5 mins
Cook time: 15 - 20 mins
Serves: 4

Ingredients:

- 1 head of cauliflower, cut into 2 cm steaks
- 1 teaspoon of cumin
- Salt and pepper, to taste
- 2 tablespoons of olive oil
- 1 teaspoon of smoked paprika

Preparation Instructions:

1. Preheat the air fryer to 180 °C.
2. In a small bowl, mix together the olive oil, cumin, smoked paprika, salt and pepper.
3. Brush the cauliflower steaks with the mixture and place them in the air fryer.
4. Cook for 15-20 minutes, or until tender and golden brown, turning halfway through.
5. Remove from the air fryer and serve as a main dish.

Portobello Mushrooms

Prep time: 5 mins
Cook time: 8 - 10 mins
Serves: 4

Ingredients:

- 4 large portobello mushrooms, stems removed
- 2 cloves of garlic, minced
- Salt and pepper, to taste
- 2 tablespoons of olive oil
- 1 teaspoon of dried thyme

Preparation Instructions:

1. Preheat the air fryer to 180 °C.
2. In a small bowl, mix together the olive oil, minced garlic, dried thyme, salt and pepper.
3. Brush the mixture over the portobello mushrooms, making sure to coat them evenly.
4. Place the mushrooms in the air fryer, gill side up.
5. Cook for 8-10 minutes, or until tender and golden brown.
6. Remove from the air fryer and serve as a main dish.

Pakoras

Prep time: 10 mins
Cook time: 8 - 10 mins
Serves: 4

Ingredients:

- 250g gram flour
- 1 teaspoon of coriander powder
- 1/2 teaspoon of red chili powder
- Water, as needed
- 250g mixed vegetables (such as onions, peppers, carrots, and cauliflower), cut into small pieces
- 1 teaspoon of cumin powder
- 1 teaspoon of ginger powder
- Salt, to taste
- Oil, for brushing

Preparation Instructions:

1. Preheat the air fryer to 180 °C.
2. In a large mixing bowl, combine the gram flour, cumin powder, coriander powder, ginger powder, red chili powder and salt. Slowly add enough water to make a thick batter. The consistency should be thick enough to coat the vegetables.
3. Dip the vegetables into the batter, making sure they are well coated.
4. Place the battered vegetables in the air fryer and brush them with a little oil.
5. Cook for 8-10 minutes or until golden brown and crispy.
6. Remove from the air fryer and drain on a paper towel.
7. Serve hot with your favourite dipping sauce.

Falafel

Prep time: 10 mins
Cook time: 8 - 10 mins
Serves: 4

Ingredients:

- 250g dried chickpeas, soaked overnight and drained
- 2 cloves of garlic, minced
- 1/4 cup of fresh coriander, chopped
- 1 teaspoon of coriander powder
- Oil, for brushing
- 1 onion, chopped
- 1/4 cup of fresh parsley, chopped
- 1 teaspoon of cumin powder
- Salt and pepper, to taste

Preparation Instructions:

1. Preheat the air fryer to 180 °C.
2. In a food processor, pulse together the soaked chickpeas, onion, garlic, parsley, coriander, cumin powder, coriander powder, salt and pepper until well combined and forms a paste.
3. Form the mixture into small balls or patties.
4. Brush the falafel with a little oil and place them in the air fryer.
5. Cook for 8-10 minutes or until golden brown and crispy.
6. Remove from the air fryer and drain on a paper towel.
7. Serve hot with your favourite dipping sauce

Parmesan Aubergine

Prep time: 30 + mins
Cook time: 20 mins
Serves: 4

Ingredients:

- 2 aubergines, sliced into ½ cm rounds
- 125 g flour
- 100 g breadcrumbs
- 240 g marinara sauce
- Salt and pepper, to taste
- 2 eggs, beaten
- 100 g grated Parmesan cheese
- 120 g shredded mozzarella cheese

Preparation Instructions:

1. Preheat the air fryer to 180 °C.
2. Place the aubergine slices on a baking sheet and sprinkle with salt and pepper. Allow to sit for 30 minutes to release excess moisture.
3. Place the flour in a shallow dish, the beaten eggs in a second dish, and the breadcrumbs in a third dish.
4. Dip the aubergine slices in flour, then eggs, and finally in breadcrumbs, pressing the breadcrumbs onto the aubergine to make sure they stick.

5. Place the breaded aubergine slices in the air fryer and cook for 8-10 minutes or until golden brown.
6. Remove from the air fryer and drain on a paper towel.
7. In a baking dish, layer the cooked aubergine slices, marinara sauce, Parmesan cheese and mozzarella cheese.
8. Place the dish back in the air fryer and cook for another 5-7 minutes or until the cheese is melted and bubbly.
9. Remove from the air fryer and let it sit for a few minutes before serving.

Vegetable Kebabs

Prep time: 10 mins
Cook time: 10 mins
Serves: 4

Ingredients:

- 250g mixed vegetables (such as peppers, onions, mushrooms, and cherry tomatoes), cut into bite-size pieces
- 2 tablespoons of olive oil
- 1 teaspoon of dried oregano
- 1 teaspoon of dried thyme
- Salt and pepper, to taste

Preparation Instructions:

1. Preheat the air fryer to 180 °C.
2. In a small bowl, mix together the olive oil, oregano, thyme, salt, and pepper.
3. Thread the vegetables onto skewers, alternating between different types of vegetables.
4. Brush the skewers with the olive oil mixture.
5. Place the skewers in the air fryer.
6. Cook for 8-10 minutes, or until the vegetables are tender and slightly charred, turning halfway through.

Crunchy Fried Okra

Prep time: 5 minutes
Cook time: 8 to 10 minutes
Serves 4

Ingredients:

- 235 ml self-raising yellow cornmeal (alternatively add 1 tablespoon baking powder to cornmeal)
- 1 teaspoon Italian-style seasoning
- 1 teaspoon paprika
- 1 teaspoon salt
- ½ teaspoon freshly ground black pepper
- 2 large eggs, beaten
- 475 ml okra slices
- Cooking spray

Preparation Instructions:

1. Preheat the air fryer to 204°C. Line the air fryer basket with parchment paper.
2. In a shallow bowl, whisk the cornmeal, Italian-style seasoning, paprika, salt, and pepper until blended.
3. Place the beaten eggs in a second shallow bowl. Add the okra to the beaten egg and stir to coat.
4. Add the egg and okra mixture to the cornmeal mixture and stir until coated.
5. Place the okra on the parchment and spritz it with oil. Air fry for 4 minutes.
6. Shake the basket, spritz the okra with oil, and air fry for 4 to 6 minutes more until lightly browned and crispy.
7. Serve immediately.

Veggie Fried Rice

Prep time: 10 mins
Cook time: 10 mins
Serves: 4

Ingredients:

- 2 tablespoons of oil
- 2 cloves of garlic, minced
- 150 g mixed vegetables (such as peas, carrots, corn, and peppers), diced
- 2 eggs, beaten
- Salt and pepper, to taste
- 1 onion, diced
- 400 g cooked rice
- 2 tablespoons of soy sauce

Preparation Instructions:

1. Preheat the air fryer to 180 °C.
2. In a pan or wok, heat the oil and sauté the onion and garlic until softened.
3. Add the rice and vegetables and stir-fry for 2-3 minutes.
4. Push the rice mixture to the side of the pan and pour the beaten eggs in the centre. Scramble the eggs and then mix them with the rice mixture.
5. Stir in the soy sauce, salt and pepper.
6. Line the airfryer basket with some parchment paper.
7. Place the rice mixture in the air fryer and cook for 8-10 minutes, or until heated through and crispy.
8. Remove from the air fryer and serve.

Asian Style Tofu Kebabs

Prep time: 30 + mins
Cook time: 15 - 20 mins
Serves: 4

Ingredients:

- 400g extra-firm tofu, drained and pressed
- 2 tablespoons of hoisin sauce
- 1 teaspoon of grated ginger
- 1 tablespoon of cornflour
- Oil, for brushing

- 2 tablespoons of soy sauce
- 2 cloves of garlic, minced
- 1 teaspoon of sesame oil
- Salt and pepper, to taste

Preparation Instructions:

1. Preheat the air fryer to 180 °C.
2. In a small bowl, mix together the soy sauce, hoisin sauce, minced garlic, grated ginger, sesame oil, cornflour, salt and pepper.
3. Cut the tofu into cubes and place them in a large resealable bag. Pour the marinade over the tofu and toss to coat. Let it marinate for at least 30 minutes or overnight in the refrigerator.
4. Thread the tofu cubes onto skewers.
5. Brush the skewers with a little oil and place them in the air fryer.
6. Cook for 15-20 minutes, or until crispy and golden brown, turning halfway through.
7. Remove from the air fryer and serve with your favourite dipping sauce.

Stuffed Peppers

Prep time: 10 mins
Cook time: 20 mins
Serves: 4

Ingredients:

- 4 peppers, halved lengthwise and seeded
- 250g cooked black beans
- 2 cloves of garlic, minced
- 1 teaspoon of smoked paprika
- 50 g shredded cheddar cheese

- 250g cooked quinoa
- 1 red onion, diced
- 1 teaspoon of cumin powder
- Salt and pepper, to taste

Preparation Instructions:

1. Preheat the air fryer to 180 °C.
2. In a mixing bowl, combine the cooked quinoa, black beans, onion, garlic, cumin, smoked paprika, salt, and pepper.
3. Stuff the pepper halves with the quinoa mixture and place them in the air fryer.
4. Cook for 15-20 minutes or until the peppers are tender.
5. Remove from the air fryer, top with shredded cheese and cook for another 2-3 minutes or until cheese is melted.

Asparagus Fries

Prep time: 15 minutes
Cook time: 5 to 7 minutes per batch
Serves 4

Ingredients:

- 340 g fresh asparagus spears with tough ends trimmed off
- 2 egg whites
- 60 ml water
- 95 g Panko bread crumbs
- 60 g grated Parmesan cheese, plus 2 tablespoons
- ¼ teaspoon salt
- Oil for misting or cooking spray

Preparation Instructions:

1. Preheat the air fryer to 200ºC.
2. In a shallow dish, beat egg whites and water until slightly foamy.
3. In another shallow dish, combine panko, Parmesan, and salt.
4. Dip asparagus spears in egg, then roll in crumbs. Spray with oil or cooking spray.
5. Place a layer of asparagus in air fryer basket, leaving just a little space in between each spear. Stack another layer on top, crosswise. Air fry at 200ºC for 5 to 7 minutes, until crispy and golden brown.
6. Repeat to cook remaining asparagus.

Cauliflower Buffalo Wings

Prep time: 5 - 10 mins
Cook time: 25 mins
Serves: 4

Ingredients:

- 1 head of cauliflower, cut into florets
- 60 g flour
- 1/2 teaspoon of garlic powder
- 1/2 teaspoon of onion powder
- Salt and pepper, to taste
- 120 ml hot sauce
- 2 tablespoons of butter, melted
- Blue cheese dressing, for dipping

Preparation Instructions:

1. Preheat the air fryer to 180 °C.
2. In a large mixing bowl, combine the flour, garlic powder, onion powder, salt, and pepper.
3. Dip the cauliflower florets in the flour mixture, making sure they are well coated.
4. Place the cauliflower florets in the air fryer and cook for 15-20 minutes or until tender and crispy.
5. Remove from the air fryer and toss in the hot sauce and melted butter.
6. Place the cauliflower florets back in the air fryer and cook for another 2-3 minutes.
7. Remove from the air fryer and serve with blue cheese dressing.

Chapter 6   Vegetarian Vegetables and Sides

Chickpea and Sweet Potato Fritters

Prep time: 10 mins
Cook time: 10 mins
Serves: 4

Ingredients:

- 1 can of chickpeas, drained and rinsed
- 30 g flour
- 1 tablespoon of cumin powder
- 1/2 teaspoon of baking powder
- Oil, for brushing
- 1 sweet potato, peeled and grated
- 30 g polenta
- 1 teaspoon of coriander powder
- Salt and pepper, to taste

Preparation Instructions:

1. Preheat the air fryer to 180 °C.
2. In a food processor, pulse together the chickpeas, sweet potato, flour, polenta, cumin powder, coriander powder, baking powder, salt and pepper until a thick paste forms.
3. Form the mixture into small patties.
4. Brush the patties with a little oil and place them in the air fryer.
5. Cook for 8-10 minutes or until golden brown and crispy, flipping halfway through.
6. Remove from the air fryer and drain on a paper towel.

Roasted Cauliflower

Prep time: 5 mins
Cook time: 10 mins
Serves: 4 - 6

Ingredients:

- 400g cauliflower florets
- 1 teaspoon of smoked paprika
- 2 tablespoons of olive oil
- Salt and pepper, to taste

Preparation Instructions:

1. Preheat the air fryer to 180 °C.
2. In a large mixing bowl, toss the cauliflower florets with olive oil, smoked paprika, salt and pepper.
3. Place the cauliflower florets in the air fryer and cook for 8-10 minutes or until tender and crispy, flipping halfway through.
4. Remove from the air fryer and serve as a side dish or as a topping for salads or bowls.

Garlic Parmesan Brussel Sprouts

Prep time: 5 mins
Cook time: 10 mins
Serves: 4 - 6

Ingredients:

- 400g Brussels sprouts, trimmed and halved
- 2 cloves of garlic, minced
- Salt and pepper, to taste
- 2 tablespoons of olive oil
- 2 tablespoons of grated Parmesan cheese

Preparation Instructions:

1. Preheat the air fryer to 180 °C.
2. In a large mixing bowl, toss the Brussels sprouts with olive oil, minced garlic, grated Parmesan cheese, salt, and pepper.
3. Place the Brussels sprouts in the air fryer and cook for 8-10 minutes or until tender and crispy, flipping halfway through.
4. Remove from the air fryer and serve as a side dish.

Sweet Potato Fries

Prep time: 5 mins
Cook time: 10 - 15 mins
Serves: 4 - 6

Ingredients:

- 600g sweet potatoes, peeled and cut into fries
- 1 teaspoon of smoked paprika
- 2 tablespoons of olive oil
- Salt and pepper, to taste

Preparation Instructions:

1. Preheat the air fryer to 180 °C.
2. In a large mixing bowl, toss the sweet potato fries with olive oil, smoked paprika, salt, and pepper.
3. Place the sweet potato fries in the air fryer and cook for 10 -15 minutes or until tender and crispy, flipping halfway through.
4. Remove from the air fryer and serve as a side dish.

Air Fryer Baked Courgette

Prep time: 5 mins
Cook time: 8- 10 mins
Serves: 4 - 6

Ingredients:

- 2 courgettes, sliced
- 1 teaspoon of dried basil
- 2 tablespoons of olive oil
- Salt and pepper, to taste

Preparation Instructions:

1. Preheat the air fryer to 180 °C.
2. In a large mixing bowl, toss the courgette slices with olive oil, dried basil, salt, and pepper.
3. Place the courgette slices in the air fryer and cook for 8-10 minutes or until tender and slightly charred, flipping halfway through.
4. Remove from the air fryer and serve as a side dish or as a topping for salads or bowls.

Air Fryer Baked Butternut Squash

Prep time: 5 mins
Cook time: 10 -15 mins
Serves: 4 - 6

Ingredients:

- 400g butternut squash, peeled and diced
- 1 teaspoon of cinnamon powder
- 1 tablespoon of olive oil
- Salt and pepper, to taste

Preparation Instructions:

1. Preheat the air fryer to 180 °C.
2. In a large mixing bowl, toss the butternut squash with olive oil, cinnamon powder, salt, and pepper.
3. Place the butternut squash in the air fryer and cook for 10 -15 minutes or until tender and slightly charred, flipping halfway through.
4. Remove from the air fryer and serve as a side dish.

Air Fryer Roasted Beetroot

Prep time: 5 mins
Cook time: 8 -10 mins
Serves: 4 - 6

Ingredients:

- 400g beetroot, peeled and diced
- 1 teaspoon of dried rosemary
- 2 tablespoons of olive oil
- Salt and pepper, to taste

Preparation Instructions:

1. Preheat the air fryer to 180 °C.
2. In a large mixing bowl, toss the beets with olive oil, dried rosemary, salt, and pepper.
3. Place the beets in the air fryer and cook for 8-10 minutes or until tender and slightly charred,

flipping halfway through.

    4. Remove from the air fryer and serve as a side dish.

Aubergine Fries

Prep time: 5 mins

Cook time: 8 -10 mins

Serves: 4 - 6

Ingredients:

- 2 medium aubergines
- 100 g breadcrumbs
- Salt and pepper, to taste
- 60 g flour
- 1 teaspoon of dried thyme
- Oil, for brushing
- 2 large eggs, beaten

Preparation Instructions:

1. Preheat the air fryer to 180 °C.
2. Cut the aubergineinto fries shape.
3. Place the flour, beaten eggs, and breadcrumbs in separate shallow dishes.
4. Mix thyme, salt and pepper in the breadcrumbs.
5. Dip the aubergine fries into the flour, then the beaten eggs, and finally the breadcrumbs mixture, pressing the breadcrumbs onto the aubergine to adhere.
6. Brush the aubergine fries with a little oil and place them in the air fryer.
7. Cook for 8-10 minutes or until golden brown and crispy, turning halfway through.

Air Fryer Roasted Vegetables

Prep time: 5 mins

Cook time: 10- 15 mins

Serves: 4 - 6

Ingredients:

- 400g vegetables of your choice (e.g. peppers, courgette, aubergine, onion, carrot, broccoli, cauliflower)
- 2 tablespoons of olive oil
- Salt and pepper, to taste
- 1 teaspoon of dried herbs of your choice (e.g. rosemary, thyme, oregano)

Preparation Instructions:

1. Preheat the air fryer to 180 °C.
2. Cut the vegetables into bite-size pieces.
3. In a large mixing bowl, toss the vegetables with olive oil, dried herbs, salt, and pepper.
4. Place the vegetables in the air fryer and cook for 10-15 minutes or until tender and slightly charred, flipping halfway through.

Zesty Parmesan Asparagus

Prep time: 5 mins
Cook time: 8 - 10 mins
Serves: 4 - 6

Ingredients:

- 400g asparagus, trimmed
- 1 teaspoon of lemon zest
- 2 tablespoons of grated Parmesan cheese
- 2 tablespoons of olive oil
- 1 tablespoon of lemon juice
- Salt and pepper, to taste

Preparation Instructions:

1. Preheat the air fryer to 180 °C.
2. In a large mixing bowl, toss the asparagus with olive oil, lemon zest, lemon juice, grated Parmesan cheese, salt, and pepper.
3. Place the asparagus in the air fryer and cook for 8-10 minutes or until tender and slightly charred, flipping halfway through.

Air Fryer Mushroom and Onions

Prep time: 5 mins
Cook time: 8 - 10 mins
Serves: 4 - 6

Ingredients:

- 250g of mushrooms, sliced
- 1 teaspoon of dried thyme
- 1 onion, sliced
- Salt and pepper, to taste
- 2 tablespoons of olive oil

Preparation Instructions:

1. Preheat the air fryer to 180 °C.
2. In a large mixing bowl, toss the mushrooms and onion with olive oil, dried thyme, salt, and pepper.
3. Place the mushrooms and onion in the air fryer and cook for 8-10 minutes or until tender and slightly charred, flipping halfway through.
4. Remove from the air fryer and serve as a side dish or as a topping for salads or bowls.

Lush Vegetable Salad

Prep time: 15 minutes
Cook time: 10 minutes
Serves 4

Ingredients:

- 6 plum tomatoes, halved
- 2 large red onions, sliced
- 4 long red pepper, sliced

- 2 yellow pepper, sliced
- 6 cloves garlic, crushed
- 1 tablespoon extra-virgin olive oil
- 1 teaspoon paprika
- ½ lemon, juiced
- Salt and ground black pepper, to taste
- 1 tablespoon baby capers

Preparation Instructions:

1. Preheat the air fryer to 220ºC.
2. Put the tomatoes, onions, peppers, and garlic in a large bowl and cover with the extra-virgin olive oil, paprika, and lemon juice. Sprinkle with salt and pepper as desired.
3. Line the inside of the air fryer basket with aluminum foil. Put the vegetables inside and air fry for 10 minutes, ensuring the edges turn brown.
4. Serve in a salad bowl with the baby capers.

Crispy Kale

Prep time: 5 mins
Cook time: 5 - 8 mins
Serves: 4

Ingredients:

- 1 bunch of kale, washed and dried
- 2 tablespoons of olive oil
- 1 teaspoon of garlic powder
- Salt and pepper, to taste

Preparation Instructions:

1. Preheat the air fryer to 180 ºC.
2. Remove the kale leaves from the thick stem, and tear into bite-size pieces.
3. In a large mixing bowl, toss the kale with olive oil, garlic powder, salt, and pepper.
4. Place the kale in the air fryer and cook for 5-8 minutes or until crispy and slightly charred, flipping halfway through.

'Roasted' Peppers

Prep time: 5 mins
Cook time: 8 - 10 mins
Serves: 4 - 6

Ingredients:

- 400g peppers, seeded and sliced
- 2 tablespoons of olive oil
- 1 teaspoon of smoked paprika
- Salt and pepper, to taste

Preparation Instructions:

1. Preheat the air fryer to 180 ºC.
2. In a large mixing bowl, toss the peppers with olive oil, smoked paprika, salt, and pepper.
3. Place the bell peppers in the air fryer and cook for 8-10 minutes or until tender and slightly charred, flipping halfway through.

Chapter 7 Beans and Grains

Quinoa and Black Bean Cakes

Prep time: 5 mins

Cook time: 8 - 10 mins

Serves: 4 - 6

Ingredients:

- 200g of cooked quinoa
- 100g of diced onions
- 2 cloves of garlic, minced
- 30g of olive oil
- 400g can of black beans, drained and rinsed
- 100g of diced peppers
- 1 egg
- Salt and pepper, to taste
- 60g of chopped coriander
- 100g of breadcrumbs

Preparation Instructions:

1. Preheat the air fryer to 180 °C.
2. In a large mixing bowl, mash the black beans with a fork or a potato masher.
3. Add the cooked quinoa, onions,peppers, coriander, garlic, egg, breadcrumbs, salt, and pepper.
4. Mix until well combined.
5. Shape the mixture into cakes.
6. In a large mixing bowl, toss the cakes with olive oil.
7. Place the cakes in the air fryer and cook for 8-10 minutes or until golden brown and crispy, flipping halfway through.

Chickpea and Brown Rice Cakes

Prep time: 5 mins

Cook time: 8 - 10 mins

Serves: 4 - 6

Ingredients:

- 200g of cooked brown rice
- 100g of diced carrots
- 2 cloves of garlic, minced
- 30g of olive oil
- 400g can of chickpeas, drained and rinsed
- 100g of diced celery
- 1 egg
- Salt and pepper, to taste
- 60g of chopped parsley
- 100g of breadcrumbs

Preparation Instructions:

1. Preheat the air fryer to 180 °C.
2. In a large mixing bowl, mash the chickpeas with a fork or a potato masher.
3. Add the cooked brown rice, carrots, celery, parsley, garlic, egg, breadcrumbs, salt, and pepper. Mix until well combined.
4. Shape the mixture into cakes.

5. In a small bowl, mix the olive oil.

6. Brush the cakes with the oil mixture

7. Place the cakes in the air fryer and cook for 8-10 minutes or until golden brown and crispy, flipping halfway through.

Lentil and Barley Cakes

Prep time: 5 mins

Cook time: 8 - 10 mins

Serves: 4 - 6

Ingredients:

- 200g of cooked barley
- 100g of diced onion
- 2 cloves of garlic, minced
- 30g of olive oil

- 400g can of lentils, drained and rinsed
- 100g of diced mushrooms
- 1 egg
- Salt and pepper, to taste

- 60g of chopped coriander
- 100g of breadcrumbs

Preparation Instructions:

1. Preheat the air fryer to 180 °C.

2. In a large mixing bowl, mash the lentils with a fork or a potato masher.

3. Add the cooked barley, onion, mushrooms, coriander, garlic, egg, breadcrumbs, salt, and pepper. Mix until well combined.

4. Shape the mixture into cakes.

5. In a small bowl, mix the olive oil.

6. Brush the cakes with the oil mixture

7. Place the cakes in the air fryer and cook for 8-10 minutes or until golden brown and crispy, flipping halfway through.

Blackbean and Quinoa Burrito Bowl

Prep time: 5 mins

Cook time: 8 - 10 mins

Serves: 4

Ingredients:

- 200g of cooked quinoa
- 100g of diced peppers
- 60g of diced onions
- 60 g salsa
- 25 g shredded cheddar cheese

- 400g can of black beans, drained and rinsed
- 100g of diced tomatoes
- 2 cloves of garlic, minced
- 60 g sour cream
- Salt and pepper, to taste

Preparation Instructions:

1. Preheat the air fryer to 180 °C.

2. In a large mixing bowl, combine the cooked quinoa, black beans, peppers, tomatoes, onions, garlic, salsa, sour cream, cheese, salt and pepper. Mix until well combined.
3. Place the mixture in the air fryer and cook for 8-10 minutes or until heated through and cheese is melted.
4. Remove from the air fryer and serve as a main dish.
5. You can also add some other herbs or spices like thyme, oregano or cumin powder to suit your taste.
6. You can also add any other toppings like avocado, lettuce, or coriander for more flavour and texture.

Chickpea and Millet Fritters

Prep time: 5 mins
Cook time: 8 - 10 mins
Serves: 4

Ingredients:

- 200g of cooked millet
- 100g of grated carrots
- 2 cloves of minced garlic
- 30g of olive oil
- 400g can of chickpeas, drained and rinsed
- 100g of grated courgette
- 1 egg
- Salt and pepper, to taste
- 60g of chopped parsley
- 100g of breadcrumbs

Preparation Instructions:

1. Preheat the air fryer to 180 °C.
2. In a large mixing bowl, mash the chickpeas with a fork or a potato masher.
3. Add the cooked millet, grated carrots, courgette, parsley, garlic, egg, breadcrumbs, salt
4. Shape the mixture into small fritters.
5. In a small bowl, mix the olive oil.
6. Brush the fritters with the oil mixture
7. Place the fritters in the air fryer and cook for 8-10 minutes or until golden brown and crispy, flipping halfway through.

Brown Rice and Vegetable Pilaf

Prep time: 5 mins
Cook time: 8 - 10 mins
Serves: 4

Ingredients:

- 200g of cooked brown rice
- 100g of diced onion
- 2 tablespoons of olive oil
- 100g of diced carrots
- 60g of chopped parsley
- Salt and pepper, to taste
- 100g of diced celery
- 2 cloves of minced garlic

Preparation Instructions:

1. Preheat the air fryer to 180 °C.
2. In a large mixing bowl, combine the cooked brown rice, carrots, celery, onion, parsley, garlic, olive oil, salt and pepper. Mix until well combined.
3. Place the mixture in a lined air fryer and cook for 8-10 minutes or until the vegetables are tender and the rice is heated through.
4. Remove from the air fryer and serve.

Barley and Vegetable Casserole

Prep time: 5 mins
Cook time: 20 - 25 mins
Serves: 4

Ingredients:

- 200g of cooked barley
- 100g of diced carrots
- 100g of diced celery
- 100g of diced onion
- 60g of chopped parsley
- 2 cloves of minced garlic
- 2 tablespoons of olive oil
- 25 g grated Cheddar cheese
- Salt and pepper, to taste

Preparation Instructions:

1. Preheat the air fryer to 180 °C.
2. In a large mixing bowl, combine the cooked barley, carrots, celery, onion, parsley, garlic, olive oil, Cheddar cheese, salt and pepper. Mix until well combined.
3. Transfer the mixture into a casserole dish that fits in the air fryer and press down the mixture to make it even.
4. Place the casserole dish in the air fryer and cook for 20-25 minutes or until the vegetables are tender and the cheese is melted and golden brown.
5. Remove from the air fryer and let it cool for a few minutes before serving.

Spelt and Vegetable Bake

Prep time: 5 mins
Cook time: 20 - 25 mins
Serves: 4

Ingredients:

- 200g of cooked spelt
- 100g of diced butternut squash
- 100g of diced courgette
- 100g of diced onion
- 2 cloves of minced garlic
- 2 tablespoons of olive oil
- 30 g grated mozzarella cheese
- Salt and pepper, to taste

Preparation Instructions:

1. Preheat the air fryer to 180 °C.
2. In a large mixing bowl, combine the cooked spelt, butternut squash, courgette, onion, garlic,

olive oil, mozzarella cheese, salt and pepper. Mix until well combined.

3. Transfer the mixture into a baking dish that fits in the air fryer and press down the mixture to make it even.

4. Place the baking dish in the air fryer and cook for 20-25 minutes or until the vegetables are tender and the cheese is melted and golden brown.

5. Remove from the air fryer and let it cool for a few minutes before serving.

White Bean and Kale Salad

Prep time: 5 mins
Cook time: 8 - 10 mins
Serves: 4

Ingredients:

- 400g can of white beans, drained and rinsed
- 100g of chopped kale
- 100g of diced tomatoes
- 60g of diced red onion
- 2 cloves of minced garlic
- 2 tablespoons of olive oil
- 2 tablespoons of lemon juice
- Salt and pepper, to taste

Preparation Instructions:

1. Preheat the air fryer to 180 ℃.

2. In a large mixing bowl, combine the white beans, kale, tomatoes, red onion, garlic, olive oil, lemon juice, salt and pepper. Mix until well combined.

3. Place the mixture in the air fryer and cook for 8-10 minutes or until the kale is wilted and the salad is heated through.

4. Remove from the air fryer and let it cool for a few minutes before serving.

Bean Burgers

Prep time: 5 mins
Cook time: 8 - 10 mins
Serves: 4 - 6

Ingredients:

- 400g can of black beans, drained and rinsed
- 100g of diced peppers
- 100g of diced onion
- 60g of chopped coriander
- 2 cloves of minced garlic
- 2 tablespoons of flour (can use gluten-free flour)
- 2 tablespoons of olive oil
- Salt and pepper, to taste

Preparation Instructions:

1. Preheat the air fryer to 180 ℃.

2. In a large mixing bowl, mash the black beans with a fork or a potato masher.

3. Add the diced peppers, onion, coriander, garlic, flour, olive oil, salt and pepper. Mix until well combined.

4. Form the mixture into patties of your desired size.
5. Place the patties in the air fryer and cook for 8-10 minutes or until the patties are golden brown and crispy, flipping halfway through.

Classic Jacket Potato (Beans & Cheese)

Prep time: 5 minutes
Cook time: 50 minutes
Serves 4

Ingredients:

- 4 large potatoes
- 1 tsp chilli flakes (optional)
- 60g butter (4 tbsp)
- 500g baked beans
- 1 tsp ground black pepper (optional)
- 180g cheddar cheese

Preparation Instructions:

1. Preheat the air fryer at 180° for 5 minutes
2. Make multiple insertions in the potato with a fork, ensuring they do not burst whilst baking
3. Place the potatoes into the air fryer and select the 'bake/roast' function at 200° for 50 minutes (if applicable)
4. Meanwhile, place the baked beans in the microwave or cooking pan for 2 minutes
5. Retrieve the potatoes and cut down the centre of the potatoes
6. Plate the potatoes up and layer a tbsp of butter in the centres
7. Divide the baked beans by 4 and dollop them in the centre of each potato
8. Top the hot baked beans with cheese, which should melt it partially
9. Season the potatoes with ground black pepper, chilli flakes (optional) and then serve

Chickpea and Vegetable Patties

Prep time: 5 mins
Cook time: 8 - 10 mins
Serves: 4 - 6

Ingredients:

- 400g can of chickpeas, drained and rinsed
- 100g of grated courgette
- 2 tablespoons of flour (can use gluten-free flour)
- Salt and pepper, to taste
- 100g of grated carrots
- 60g of chopped parsley
- 2 cloves of minced garlic
- 2 tablespoons of olive oil

Preparation Instructions:

1. Preheat the air fryer to 180 °C.
2. In a large mixing bowl, mash the chickpeas with a fork or a potato masher.
3. Add the grated carrots, courgette, parsley, garlic, flour, olive oil, salt and pepper. Mix until well combined.

4. Form the mixture into patties of your desired size.

5. Place the patties in the air fryer and cook for 8-10 minutes or until the patties are golden brown and crispy, flipping halfway through.

White Bean and Spinach Stuffed Mushrooms

Prep time: 5 mins

Cook time: 12 - 15 mins

Serves: 4

Ingredients:

- 4 large Portobello mushrooms
- 100g of chopped spinach
- 2 cloves of minced garlic
- 2 tablespoons of breadcrumbs
- 400g can of white beans, drained and rinsed
- 100g of diced onion
- 2 tablespoons of olive oil
- Salt and pepper, to taste

Preparation Instructions:

1. Preheat the air fryer to 180 °C.

2. Remove the stems from the Portobello mushrooms and scrape out the gills with a spoon.

3. In a large mixing bowl, mash the white beans with a fork or a potato masher.

4. Add the chopped spinach, onion, garlic, olive oil, breadcrumbs, salt and pepper. Mix until well combined.

5. Stuff the mushroom caps with the bean mixture, packing it tightly.

6. Place the stuffed mushrooms in the air fryer and cook for 12-15 minutes or until the mushrooms are tender and the filling is heated through.

Black Bean and Sweet Potato Enchiladas

Prep time: 5 mins

Cook time: 8 - 10 mins

Serves: 4

Ingredients:

- 400g can of black beans, drained and rinsed
- 100g of diced onion
- 2 tablespoons of olive oil
- Salt and pepper, to taste
- 100g of diced sweet potatoes
- 100g of diced pepper
- 2 cloves of minced garlic
- 2 tablespoons of enchilada sauce
- 8 corn tortillas

Preparation Instructions:

1. Preheat the air fryer to 180 °C.

2. In a large mixing bowl, mash the black beans with a fork or a potato masher.

3. Add the diced sweet potatoes, onion, pepper, garlic, olive oil, enchilada sauce, salt and pepper. Mix until well combined.

4. Place a spoonful of the mixture on each tortilla and roll it tightly.

5. Place the enchiladas in the air fryer and cook for 8-10 minutes or until the enchiladas are heated through and the tortillas are crispy, flipping halfway through.

6. Remove from the air fryer and let it cool for a few minutes before serving.

Farro and Vegetable Salad

Prep time: 5 mins

Cook time: 8 - 10 mins

Serves: 4

Ingredients:

- 200g of cooked farro
- 100g of diced tomatoes
- 100g of diced cucumber
- 100g of diced red onion
- 60g of chopped parsley
- 2 cloves of minced garlic
- 2 tablespoons of olive oil
- 2 tablespoons of lemon juice
- Salt and pepper, to taste

Preparation Instructions:

1. Preheat the air fryer to 180 °C.

2. In a large mixing bowl, combine the cooked farro, diced tomatoes, cucumber, red onion, parsley, garlic, olive oil, lemon juice, salt and pepper. Mix until well combined.

3. Place the mixture in a lined air fryer basket and cook for 8-10 minutes or until the salad is heated through.

4. Remove from the air fryer and let it cool for a few minutes before serving.

Millet and Vegetable Croquettes

Prep time: 5 mins

Cook time: 8 - 10 mins

Serves: 4

Ingredients:

- 200g of cooked millet
- 100g of diced carrots
- 100g of diced courgette
- 100g of diced onion
- 2 cloves of minced garlic
- Salt and pepper, to taste
- 2 tablespoons of flour (can use gluten-free flour)
- 2 tablespoons of olive oil

Preparation Instructions:

1. Preheat the air fryer to 180 °C.

2. In a large mixing bowl, combine the cooked millet, diced carrots, courgette, onion, garlic, flour, olive oil, salt and pepper. Mix until well combined.

3. Form the mixture into small, cylindrical patties.

4. Place the croquettes in the air fryer and cook for 8-10 minutes or until the croquettes are golden brown and crispy, flipping halfway through.

5. Remove from the air fryer and let it cool for a few minutes before serving.

Chapter 8   Pizzas, Wraps and Sandwiches

Veggie Sandwich

Prep time: 5 mins
Cook time: 3 - 5 mins
Serves: 2

Ingredients:

- 4 slices of bread
- 100g of sliced onion
- 2 tablespoons of mayonnaise
- 100g of sliced cucumber
- 100g of sliced mushrooms
- Salt and pepper, to taste
- 100g of sliced tomatoes
- 100g of sliced avocado

Preparation Instructions:

1. Preheat the air fryer to 180 °C.
2. Spread mayonnaise on one side of each slice of bread.
3. Place the vegetables between two slices of bread and press the edges together to make a sandwich.
4. Place the sandwich in the air fryer and cook for 3-5 minutes or until the bread is golden brown and the vegetables are tender, flipping halfway through.
5. Remove from the air fryer and let it cool for a few minutes before serving.
6. You can also add any other fillings to your sandwich like cheese, hummus, or salsa for more flavour and texture.

Tuna Melt

Prep time: 5 mins
Cook time: 3 - 5 mins
Serves: 2

Ingredients:

- 200g of canned tuna, drained
- 2 tablespoons of mayonnaise
- 100g of diced celery
- 100g of grated cheddar cheese
- 100g of diced onion
- Salt and pepper, to taste

Preparation Instructions:

1. Preheat the air fryer to 180 °C.
2. In a mixing bowl, combine the canned tuna, diced celery, onion, mayonnaise, salt, and pepper. Mix until well combined.
3. Spread the tuna mixture on one slice of bread, top with grated cheese.
4. Place the sandwich in the air fryer and cook for 3-5 minutes or until the bread is golden brown and the cheese is melted, flipping halfway through.

French Dip Sandwich

Prep time: 5 mins
Cook time: 3 - 5 mins
Serves: 2

Ingredients:

- 4 slices of bread
- 2 tablespoons of beef stock
- 100g of thinly sliced roast beef
- 2 tablespoons of butter
- 2 cloves of minced garlic
- Salt and pepper, to taste

Preparation Instructions:

1. Preheat the air fryer to 180 °C.
2. Spread butter on one side of each slice of bread.
3. Place the roast beef between two slices of bread and press the edges together to make a sandwich.
4. Place the sandwich in the air fryer and cook for 3-5 minutes or until the bread is golden brown and the roast beef is heated through, flipping halfway through.
5. Remove from the air fryer and let it cool for a few minutes before serving.
6. Serve with the beef stock for dipping.

BBQ Chicken Sandwich

Prep time: 5 mins
Cook time: 3 - 5 mins
Serves: 2

Ingredients:

- 4 slices of bread
- 100g of BBQ sauce
- 2 tablespoons of butter
- 200g of cooked, shredded chicken
- 100g of grated cheddar cheese
- Salt and pepper, to taste

Preparation Instructions:

1. Preheat the air fryer to 180 °C.
2. Spread butter on one side of each slice of bread.
3. In a mixing bowl, combine the shredded chicken, BBQ sauce, salt, and pepper. Mix until well combined.
4. Spread the BBQ chicken mixture on one slice of bread, top with grated cheese.
5. Place the sandwich in the air fryer and cook for 3-5 minutes or until the bread is golden brown and the cheese is melted, flipping halfway through.

Cuban Sandwich

Prep time: 5 mins
Cook time: 3 - 5 mins
Serves: 2

Ingredients:

- 4 slices of bread
- 100g of thinly sliced ham
- 100g of dill pickles, sliced
- 2 tablespoons of butter
- 100g of thinly sliced roast pork
- 100g of thinly sliced Swiss cheese
- 2 tablespoons of yellow mustard
- Salt and pepper, to taste

Preparation Instructions:

1. Preheat the air fryer to 180 °C.
2. Spread butter on one side of each slice of bread.
3. Spread mustard on one side of the bread.
4. Place the roast pork, ham, Swiss cheese, and pickles between two slices of bread and press the edges together to make a sandwich.
5. Place the sandwich in the air fryer and cook for 3-5 minutes or until the bread is golden brown and the cheese is melted, flipping halfway through.

Falafel Sandwich

Prep time: 5 mins
Cook time: 3 - 5 mins
Serves: 2

Ingredients:

- 4 slices of pita bread
- 100g of diced tomatoes
- 2 tablespoons of lemon juice
- 200g of falafel balls
- 100g of diced cucumber
- Salt and pepper, to taste
- 100g of hummus
- 2 tablespoons of tahini

Preparation Instructions:

1. Preheat the air fryer to 180 °C.
2. Place the falafel balls in the air fryer and cook for 8-10 minutes or until golden brown and crispy.
3. While the falafel is cooking, mix together the hummus, tahini, lemon juice, salt, and pepper in a small bowl.
4. Cut the pita bread in half to create a pocket.
5. Spread the hummus mixture inside the pita bread, add the cooked falafel balls, diced tomatoes, and cucumber.
6. Place the sandwich in the air fryer and cook for 3-5 minutes or until the pita bread is warm and the falafel is heated through, flipping halfway through.

Chicken Fajita Wrap

Prep time: 5 mins
Cook time: 10 - 12 mins
Serves: 4

Ingredients:

- 4 tortilla wraps
- 200g of sliced chicken breast
- 100g of sliced peppers
- 100g of sliced onions
- 2 tablespoons of olive oil
- 1 teaspoon of chili powder
- 1 teaspoon of cumin powder
- Salt and pepper, to taste

Preparation Instructions:

1. Preheat the air fryer to 180 °C.
2. In a mixing bowl, combine the sliced chicken, peppers, onions, olive oil, chili powder, cumin powder, salt, and pepper. Mix until well combined.
3. Pla0ce the chicken and vegetable mixture in the air fryer and cook for 8-10 minutes or until the chicken is cooked through and the vegetables are tender, flipping halfway through.
4. Remove from the air fryer and let it cool for a few minutes before serving.
5. Place the cooked chicken and vegetables in the center of each tortilla wrap and roll them up tightly.
6. Place the wraps in the air fryer and cook for 2-3 minutes or until the tortilla is golden brown and crispy.

Vegetable Wrap

Prep time: 5 mins
Cook time: 10 - 12 mins
Serves: 4

Ingredients:

- 4 tortilla wraps
- 100g of sliced carrots
- 100g of sliced courgette
- 100g of sliced peppers
- 100g of sliced mushrooms
- 2 tablespoons of olive oil
- Salt and pepper, to taste

Preparation Instructions:

1. Preheat the air fryer to 180 °C.
2. In a mixing bowl, combine the sliced carrots, courgette, peppers, mushrooms, olive oil, salt, and pepper. Mix until well combined.
3. Place the vegetable mixture in the air fryer and cook for 8-10 minutes or until the vegetables are tender, flipping halfway through.
4. Remove from the air fryer and let it cool for a few minutes before serving.
5. Place the cooked vegetables in the center of each tortilla wrap and roll them up tightly.

6. Place the wraps in the air fryer and cook for 2-3 minutes or until the tortilla is golden brown and crispy.

Greek Wrap

Prep time: 5 mins
Cook time: 2 - 3 mins
Serves: 4

Ingredients:

- 4 tortilla wraps
- 100g of diced tomatoes
- 2 tablespoons of tzatziki sauce
- 200g of cooked and shredded lamb or chicken
- 100g of diced cucumber
- 2 tablespoons of olive oil
- 100g of crumbled feta cheese
- Salt and pepper, to taste

Preparation Instructions:

1. Preheat the air fryer to 180 °C.
2. Place the cooked and shredded lamb or chicken in the centre of each tortilla wrap.
3. Top with diced tomatoes, cucumber, crumbled feta cheese, and tzatziki sauce.
4. Roll the tortilla wraps tightly and brush the tops with olive oil.
5. Place the wraps in the air fryer and cook for 2-3 minutes or until the tortilla is golden brown and crispy.

BBQ Pulled Pork Wrap

Prep time: 5 mins
Cook time: 2 - 3 mins
Serves: 4

Ingredients:

- 4 tortilla wraps
- 100g of coleslaw
- 200g of cooked and shredded pork
- 2 tablespoons of mayonnaise
- 100g of BBQ sauce
- Salt and pepper, to taste

Preparation Instructions:

1. Preheat the air fryer to 180 °C.
2. In a mixing bowl, combine the shredded pork, BBQ sauce, salt, and pepper. Mix until well combined.
3. Place the BBQ pulled pork mixture in the centre of each tortilla wrap.
4. Top with coleslaw and mayonnaise.
5. Roll the tortilla wraps tightly.
6. Place the wraps in the air fryer and cook for 2-3 minutes or until the tortilla is golden brown and crispy.

Tofu Wrap

Prep time: 5 mins
Cook time: 15 mins
Serves: 4

Ingredients:

- 4 tortilla wraps
- 100g of soy sauce
- 2 tablespoons of sesame oil
- 200g of pressed and cubed tofu
- 100g of diced vegetables (such as peppers, onions, mushrooms)
- Salt and pepper, to taste

Preparation Instructions:

1. Preheat the air fryer to 180 °C.
2. In a mixing bowl, combine the cubed tofu, soy sauce, sesame oil, salt, and pepper. Mix until well combined.
3. Place the tofu and vegetable mixture in the air fryer and cook for 8-10 minutes or until the tofu is golden brown and crispy, flipping halfway through.
4. Remove from the air fryer and let it cool for a few minutes before serving.
5. Place the cooked tofu and vegetables in the centre of each tortilla wrap and roll them up tightly.
6. Place the wraps in the air fryer and cook for 2-3 minutes or until the tortilla is golden brown and crispy.

Margherita Pizza

Prep time: 5 mins
Cook time: 10 mins
Serves: 2 - 4

Ingredients:

- 1 pre-made pizza base
- 10-15 basil leaves
- 100g of crushed tomatoes
- 1 tablespoon of olive oil
- 50g of mozzarella cheese
- Salt and pepper, to taste

Preparation Instructions:

1. Preheat the air fryer to 180 °C.
2. Place the pre-made pizza base in the air fryer and cook for 2-3 minutes or until it starts to puff up and become slightly crispy.
3. Remove the crust from the air fryer and spread the crushed tomatoes over the crust, leaving a small border around the edge.
4. Top with mozzarella cheese and basil leaves.
5. Drizzle with olive oil and season with salt and pepper.
6. Place the pizza back in the air fryer and cook for an additional 5-7 minutes or until the cheese is melted and the crust is golden brown.

7. Remove from the air fryer and let it cool for a few minutes before slicing and serving.

BBQ Chicken Pizza

Prep time: 5 mins
Cook time: 10 mins
Serves: 2 - 4

Ingredients:

- 1 pre-made pizza base
- 100g of BBQ sauce
- 100g of shredded chicken
- 100g of diced red onions
- 50g of cheddar cheese

Preparation Instructions:

1. Preheat the air fryer to 180 °C.
2. Place the pre-made pizza crust in the air fryer and cook for 2-3 minutes or until it starts to puff up and become slightly crispy.
3. Remove the crust from the air fryer and spread the BBQ sauce over the crust, leaving a small border around the edge.
4. Add shredded chicken, diced red onions and cheddar cheese on top of the BBQ sauce.
5. Place the pizza back in the air fryer and cook for an additional 5-7 minutes or until the cheese is melted and the crust is golden brown.

Calzone

Prep time: 10 mins
Cook time: 10 - 12 mins
Serves: 1 - 2

Ingredients:

- 1 batch of homemade or ready made pizza dough
- 100g of ricotta cheese
- 100g of diced pepperoni
- 100g of shredded mozzarella cheese
- 2 tablespoons of olive oil
- 1 teaspoon of Italian seasoning
- Salt and pepper, to taste

Preparation Instructions:

1. Preheat the air fryer to 180 °C.
2. Roll out the pizza dough into a large circle, about ½ cm thick.
3. In a mixing bowl, combine the ricotta cheese, pepperoni or sausage, mozzarella cheese, Italian seasoning, salt, and pepper. Mix until well combined.
4. Spread the mixture over half of the rolled out dough, leaving a 2.5 cm border around the edge.
5. Fold the other half of the dough over the filling and press the edges together to seal.
6. Brush the top of the calzone with olive oil.
7. Place the calzone in the air fryer and cook for 10-12 minutes or until the crust is golden

brown and the filling is hot.

Spinach and Ricotta Calzone

Prep time: 10 mins
Cook time: 10 - 12 mins
Serves: 1 - 2

Ingredients:

- 1 batch of homemade or ready made pizza dough
- 100g of chopped spinach
- 2 tablespoons of olive oil
- Salt and pepper, to taste
- 100g of ricotta cheese
- 50g of grated Parmesan cheese
- 1 teaspoon of garlic powder

Preparation Instructions:

1. Preheat the air fryer to 180 °C.
2. Roll out the pizza dough into a large circle, about ½ cm thick.
3. In a mixing bowl, combine the ricotta cheese, chopped spinach, Parmesan cheese, garlic powder, salt, and pepper. Mix until well combined.
4. Spread the mixture over half of the rolled out dough, leaving a 2.5 cm border around the edge.
5. Fold the other half of the dough over the filling and press the edges together to seal.
6. Brush the top of the calzone with olive oil.
7. Place the calzone in the air fryer and cook for 10-12 minutes or until the crust is golden brown and the filling is hot.
8. Remove from the air fryer and let it cool for a few minutes before slicing and serving.

Chapter 9 Staples, Sauces, Dips and Dressings

BBQ Sauce

Prep time: 5 mins
Cook time: 5 - 7 mins
Serves: 4 +

Ingredients:

- 230g of ketchup
- 30ml Worcestershire sauce
- ½ tsp garlic powder
- 60g of brown sugar
- 1 tsp mustard powder
- ¼ tsp onion powder
- 60ml apple cider vinegar
- ½ tsp smoked paprika
- Salt and pepper, to taste

Preparation Instructions:

1. Preheat the air fryer to 180 °C.
2. In a mixing bowl, combine the hot sauce, butter, white vinegar, Worcestershire sauce, garlic powder, onion powder, cayenne pepper, salt, and pepper. Mix until well combined.
3. Place the mixture in a heatproof bowl and place it in the air fryer.
4. Cook for 5-7 minutes or until the sauce thickens and the butter is melted, stirring occasionally.
5. Remove from the air fryer and let it cool for a few minutes before serving.

Glazed donuts

Prep. time: 15 mins.
Cooking time: 5 mins
Serve: 6 donuts

Ingredients

- 120 ml warm water
- 35g granulated sugar + 13 g
- Half egg yolk
- Small pinch of salt
- 120g powdered sugar
- ¾ tsp (3ml) vanilla extract
- 30 ml warm milk
- 28g unsalted butter, melted
- ½ tsp (2ml) vanilla extract
- Cooking spray
- 30 ml milk
- 1 tsp (3g) dry active yeast
- Half whole egg
- 160g all-purpose flour
- Glaze
- 7 ml golden syrup

Preparation Instructions:

1. In a large measuring cup, add warm water, warm milk (45C), dry active yeast, and 13g of granulated sugar. Let the yeast mixture froth up and rise for about 5 minutes.
2. Now in a stand mixer, add the remaining of granulated sugar, unsalted melted butter, egg, egg yolk, vanilla extract, all-purpose flour (spooned and leveled off), and salt. Then pour in the yeast mixture and pace the hook attachment on and begin mixing on low speed until the flour is incorporated into liquids.

3. Next, increase the speed to high and beat for 5 minutes, and scrape down the sides of the beater bowl. If the dough looks too sticky, add 1 tablespoon of flour at a time. Make sure to mix well and scrape down the sides of the bowl between each addition of flour. (Don't add too much flour or the donuts will be too dry. They should have a slightly sticky texture to them).

4. Now place the dough in a large greased bowl and cover with a kitchen towel or plastic wrap. Let the dough rise for about one hour or until it doubles in size.

5. When the dough is ready, punch it down to release air bubbles and transfer it to a floured surface.

6. Using a rolling pin, roll the dough out to about 1.5 cm in thickness, and using a donut cutter cut out as many donuts as you can. Then reshape the scraps and cut out some more donuts.

7. Now place the cut-out donuts on a baking sheet lined with parchment paper then cover them lightly and let them rise again for about 20-30 minutes.

8. Preheat your air fryer to 175 C and spray the air fryer basket with cooking spray and place a few donuts into the air fryer basket and spray them with some more cooking spray. Make sure that the donuts are not touching.

9. Air-fry the donuts for about 4 minutes, and repeat this process with the remaining donuts and donut holes. Then transfer the donuts onto a plate lined with paper towels.

10. To make the glaze: In a large bowl combine sugar, milk, golden syrup, and vanilla extract. While the donuts are warm dip them in the glaze and let them set on a cooling rack. The glaze sets shinier when the donuts are hot. Enjoy!

Honey Mustard Sauce

Prep time: 5 mins
Cook time: 5 - 7 mins
Serves: 4 +

Ingredients:

- 115g of dijon mustard
- ½ tsp onion powder
- 60g of honey
- ½ tsp garlic powder
- 30 ml apple cider vinegar
- Salt and pepper, to taste

Preparation Instructions:

1. Preheat the air fryer to 180 °C.
2. In a mixing bowl, combine the dijon mustard, honey, apple cider vinegar, onion powder, garlic powder, salt, and pepper. Mix until well combined.
3. Place the mixture in a heatproof bowl and place it in the air fryer.
4. Cook for 5-7 minutes or until the sauce thickens, stirring occasionally

Sweet and Sour Sauce

Prep time: 5 mins
Cook time: 5 - 7 mins
Serves: 4 +

Ingredients:

- 115ml pineapple juice
- 30ml soy sauce
- ½ tsp cornflour
- 60g brown sugar
- 1 tsp garlic powder
- Salt and pepper, to taste
- 30ml rice vinegar
- ½ tsp ginger powder

Preparation Instructions:

1. Preheat the air fryer to 180 °C.
2. In a mixing bowl, combine the pineapple juice, brown sugar, rice vinegar, soy sauce, garlic powder, ginger powder, cornflour, salt, and pepper. Mix until well combined.
3. Place the mixture in a heatproof bowl and place it in the air fryer.
4. Cook for 5-7 minutes or until the sauce thickens, stirring occasionally.

Teriyaki Sauce

Prep time: 5 mins
Cook time: 5 - 7 mins
Serves: 4 +

Ingredients:

- 115g of soy sauce
- 2 tsp garlic powder
- Salt and pepper, to taste
- 60g brown sugar
- 1 tsp ginger powder
- 30ml rice vinegar
- 1 tsp cornflour

Preparation Instructions:

1. Preheat the air fryer to 180 °C.
2. In a mixing bowl, combine the soy sauce, brown sugar, rice vinegar, garlic powder, ginger powder, cornflour, salt, and pepper. Mix until well combined.
3. Place the mixture in a heatproof bowl and place it in the air fryer.
4. Cook for 5-7 minutes or until the sauce thickens, stirring occasionally.

Parmesan Garlic Sauce

Prep time: 5 mins
Cook time: 5 - 7 mins
Serves: 4 +

Ingredients:

- 115 cream
- 1 tsp onion powder
- 60g grated Parmesan cheese
- Salt and pepper, to taste
- 2 tsp garlic powder

Preparation Instructions:

1. Preheat the air fryer to 180 °C.
2. In a mixing bowl, combine the cream, grated Parmesan cheese, garlic powder, onion powder, salt, and pepper. Mix until well combined.

3. Place the mixture in a heatproof bowl and place it in the air fryer.

4. Cook for 5-7 minutes or until the sauce thickens, stirring occasionally.

Spinach and Artichoke Dip

Prep time: 5 mins

Cook time: 5 - 7 mins

Serves: 4 +

Ingredients:

- 115g frozen spinach, thawed and drained
- 115g canned artichoke hearts, drained and chopped
- 60g cream cheese, softened
- 30g sour cream
- 15g grated Parmesan cheese
- 1 tsp garlic powder
- Salt and pepper, to taste

Preparation Instructions:

1. Preheat the air fryer to 180 °C.

2. In a mixing bowl, combine the spinach, artichoke hearts, cream cheese, sour cream, grated Parmesan cheese, garlic powder, salt, and pepper. Mix until well combined.

3. Place the mixture in a heatproof bowl and place it in the air fryer.

4. Cook for 5-7 minutes or until the dip is heated through and bubbly, stirring occasionally.

Cheesy Dip

Prep time: 5 mins

Cook time: 5 - 7 mins

Serves: 4 +

Ingredients:

- 115g grated cheddar cheese
- 60g cream cheese, softened
- 30g diced tomatoes and green chilies
- 1 tsp chili powder
- ½ tsp garlic powder
- Salt and pepper, to taste

Preparation Instructions:

1. Preheat the air fryer to 180 °C.

2. In a mixing bowl, combine the grated cheddar cheese, cream cheese, diced tomatoes and green chilies, chili powder, garlic powder, salt, and pepper. Mix until well combined.

3. Place the mixture in a heatproof bowl and place it in the air fryer.

4. Cook for 5-7 minutes or until the cheese is melted and bubbly, stirring occasionally.

Gochujang Dip

Prep time: 5 minutes

Cook time: 0 minutes

Serves 4

Ingredients:

- 2 tablespoons gochujang (Korean red pepper paste)
- 1 tablespoon toasted sesame oil
- 1 tablespoon minced garlic
- 1 tablespoon mayonnaise
- 1 tablespoon minced fresh ginger
- 1 teaspoon agave nectar

Preparation Instructions:

In a small bowl, combine the gochujang, mayonnaise, sesame oil, ginger, garlic, and agave. Stir until well combined. Use immediately or store in the refrigerator, covered, for up to 3 days.

Buffalo Cauliflower Dip

Prep time: 5 mins
Cook time: 20 mins
Serves: 4 +

Ingredients:

- 500g cauliflower florets
- 15g blue cheese crumbles
- 60g buffalo sauce
- 10g garlic powder
- 30g sour cream
- Salt and pepper, to taste

Preparation Instructions:

1. Preheat the air fryer to 180 °C.
2. In a mixing bowl, combine the cauliflower florets, buffalo sauce, garlic powder, salt and pepper. Mix until the cauliflower is well coated.
3. Place the cauliflower in the air fryer and cook for 12-15 minutes or until tender and slightly charred.
4. In a separate mixing bowl, combine the cooked cauliflower, sour cream, and blue cheese crumbles. Mix well.
5. Place the mixture back in the air fryer and cook for an additional 5-7 minutes or until heated through and the cheese is melted.

Roasted Peach and Blueberry Sauce

Prep time: 10 mins
Cook time: 12 - 15 mins
Serves: 4 +

Ingredients:

- 500g peaches, pitted and sliced
- 20g cornflour
- 250g blueberries
- 10ml lemon juice
- 80g honey
- Salt, to taste

Preparation Instructions:

1. Preheat the air fryer to 180 °C.
2. Place the peaches and blueberries in the air fryer and cook for 8-10 minutes or until the

peaches are tender and the blueberries are burst.

3. Remove the peaches and blueberries from the air fryer and let them cool for a few minutes.
4. In a medium saucepan, combine the roasted peaches, blueberries, honey, cornflour, lemon juice, and salt. Bring the mixture to a simmer and cook for 2-3 minutes or until the sauce thickens.
5. Remove the saucepan from the heat and let the sauce cool for a few minutes.
6. Serve the sauce over ice cream, pancakes, or waffles.

Roasted Garlic Dip

Prep time: 5 mins
Cook time: 5 - 7 mins
Serves: 4 +

Ingredients:

- 180g cream cheese
- 15g roasted garlic
- 60g sour cream
- 10ml lemon juice
- 30g mayonnaise
- Salt and pepper, to taste

Preparation Instructions:

1. Preheat the air fryer to 180 °C.
2. In a mixing bowl, combine cream cheese, sour cream, mayonnaise, roasted garlic, lemon juice, salt, and pepper. Mix until well combined.
3. Place the mixture in a heatproof bowl and place it in the air fryer.
4. Cook for 5-7 minutes or until the cheese is melted and bubbly, stirring occasionally.
5. Remove from the air fryer and let it cool for a few minutes before serving.
6. This roasted garlic dip can be served with crackers, bread or vegetables.

Balsamic Glaze

Prep time: 5 mins
Cook time: 15 - 20 mins
Serves: 2

Ingredients:

- 150ml balsamic vinegar
- 5g Dijon mustard
- 60g brown sugar
- ¼ tsp black pepper
- 10g honey

Preparation Instructions:

1. Preheat the air fryer to 180 °C.
2. In a small mixing bowl, combine balsamic vinegar, brown sugar, honey, Dijon mustard, and black pepper. Mix until well combined.
3. Place the mixture in a heatproof bowl and place it in the air fryer.
4. Cook for 15-20 minutes or until the glaze is thickened and reduced, stirring occasionally.

Roasted Pepper Hummus

Prep time: 10 mins
Cook time: 12 -15 mins
Serves: 4 +

Ingredients:

- 400g chickpeas, drained and rinsed
- 40ml lemon juice
- 2 red peppers, deseeded and quartered
- Salt and pepper, to taste
- 80g tahini
- 20ml olive oil

Preparation Instructions:

1. Preheat the air fryer to 180 °C.
2. Place the peppers in the air fryer and cook for 12-15 minutes or until the skin is charred and the peppers are tender.
3. Remove the peppers from the air fryer and let them cool for a few minutes before peeling off the skin.
4. In a food processor, combine the chickpeas, tahini, lemon juice, garlic, olive oil, salt, and pepper.
5. Once the peppers have cooled, add them to the food processor, and pulse until smooth.
6. Adjust seasoning to taste.
7. Serve the hummus with pita bread, crackers, or vegetables.
8. If you prefer to warm up the hummus before serving, place the hummus in a heatproof dish and put it in the air fryer at a low temperature (around 150-160 °C) for a few minutes or until it is heated through

Roasted Tomato Salsa

Prep time: 10 mins
Cook time: 12 -15 mins
Serves: 4 +

Ingredients:

- 400g cherry tomatoes
- 30g fresh coriander finely chopped
- 10ml olive oil
- 60g red onion, finely chopped
- 20ml lime juice
- Salt and pepper, to taste

Preparation Instructions:

1. Preheat the air fryer to 180 °C.
2. Place the cherry tomatoes in the air fryer and cook for 12-15 minutes or until the skin is charred and the tomatoes are tender.
3. Remove the tomatoes from the air fryer and let them cool for a few minutes.
4. In a mixing bowl, combine the roasted tomatoes, red onion, coriander, lime juice, olive oil,

salt and pepper. Mix until well combined.

5. Adjust seasoning to taste.
6. Serve the salsa with tortilla chips or as a topping for tacos or burritos.

Roasted Aubergine Dip

Prep time: 10 mins
Cook time: 12 -15 mins
Serves: 4 +

Ingredients:

- 600g aubergine
- 20g garlic, minced
- 60g tahini
- 10ml olive oil
- 30ml lemon juice
- Salt and pepper, to taste

Preparation Instructions:

1. Preheat the air fryer to 180 °C.
2. Cut the aubergine into cubes and place them in the air fryer. Cook for 12-15 minutes or until the aubergine is tender.
3. Remove the aubergine from the air fryer and let it cool for a few minutes.
4. In a food processor, combine the roasted aubergine, tahini, lemon juice, garlic, olive oil, salt, and pepper. Pulse until smooth.
5. Adjust seasoning to taste.
6. Serve the dip with pita bread, crackers, or vegetables.

Roasted Carrot Dip

Prep time: 10 mins
Cook time: 12 -15 mins
Serves: 4 +

Ingredients:

- 600g carrots, peeled and sliced
- 120g cream cheese
- 1tsp cinnamon
- 60g sour cream
- Salt and pepper, to taste
- 20g honey

Preparation Instructions:

1. Preheat the air fryer to 180 °C.
2. Place the carrots in the air fryer and cook for 12-15 minutes or until the carrots are tender.
3. Remove the carrots from the air fryer and let them cool for a few minutes.
4. In a food processor, combine the roasted carrots, cream cheese, sour cream, honey, cinnamon, salt, and pepper. Pulse until smooth.
5. Adjust seasoning to taste.

Printed in Great Britain
by Amazon

19453850R00052